CREATIVE KETO MINI WAFFLES

MIYUKI MINAMI

Copyright © 2019 Miyuki Minami

All rights reserved

No part of this publication should be reproduced or distributed in any form or by any means, electrical or mechanical or stored in a database without prior permission from the publisher.

ISBN: 978-1-693527-52-4

Published Independently

The author (Miyuki Minami aka 'Keto Diet Channel') is not a licensed practitioner, physician, or medical professional. The information presented herein is not intended to diagnose, treat, cure, or prevent any disease. Full medical clearance from a licensed physician should be obtained before beginning or modifying any diet, exercise, or lifestyle program, and physicians should be informed of all nutritional changes. The author claims no responsibility to any person or entity for any liability, loss, or damage caused or alleged to be caused directly or indirectly as a result of the use, application, or interpretation of the information presented herein.

✺ Notes ✺

✺ Stevia Powder and Liquid Stevia used in these recipes are a SweetLeaf® brand:

- SweetLeaf® Stevia Sweetener Shaker

- SweetLeaf® Sweet Drops™ Liquid Stevia

If you'd like to use other sweeteners, follow the conversion calculator below:

https://sweetleaf.com/stevia-conversion-calculator/

You can enter the amount specified in these recipes in the second one 'Amount of Stevia Powder', and then use the amount shown in 'Amount of Sugar'. However, there's no guarantee that the texture of yours will be same as mine.

✺ The waffles in these recipes are cooked with a mini waffle maker, which makes a _4 inch / 10 cm_ waffle at a time.

✺ How to clean your mini waffle maker:

As soon as you're done cooking your waffles, unplug it, place a wet paper towel, and close the lid. Let it steam, open the lid, and wipe it out with a dry paper towel.

✸ Introduction ✸

I'm Miyuki Minami, a self-taught home cook. Because I'm Japanese and English is my second language, I may need to ask you to excuse my English from time to time.

I've shared my creative low carb keto recipes through the blog called 'Keto Diet Channel' for two and a half years since 2017. I decided to shut down the blog in 2019 and then deleted all of my recipes from the blog, preparing for the shutdown. However, I didn't want to trash my recipes so easily, so I self-published the cookbook with all those recipes '**CREATIVE KETO KITCHEN: 90+ Delicious & Creative Keto Recipes**', which is on sale on many Amazon global marketplaces.

And then, the 2019 Summer Keto Mini Waffle Craze started all of a sudden. I've shared my recipes as a recipe blogger only two and a half years, but I just couldn't resist my desire to develop keto mini waffle recipes. It's like an old habit. So, I shared simple Basic and Sweet Mini Waffle recipes. However, I'm a person who likes to develop creative and unique recipes, so I continued to develop more recipes. The first creative one was '**Tiramisu**', the second '**Chocolate Heaven**', and then probably the most shared keto mini waffle recipe in 2019 '**"Cream Puffs" with Custard Filling**'. I shared two more recipes: '**Keema Curry**' and '**Lemon Dome Cake**'.

Although more recipe ideas were in my mind, I quit sharing because I knew the day of the blog shutdown was just around the corner. And then, a couple readers of my blog suggested that I publish a keto mini waffle recipes cookbook because they love my creativity. So, after a long thinking, I'm now self-publishing this cookbook, featuring only Keto Mini Waffle recipes.

I put together this cookbook only with 26 recipes of mine. However, I'm only one person and they are totally my original recipes, so I believe I did a pretty good job in such a short amount of time. My fridge is still filled with mini waffles as I'm writing this.

I hope you enjoy my Keto Mini Waffle recipes!

✂ If you want to watch my demonstration videos of the above-mentioned five creative keto waffle recipes, they can be found on the following sites:

<u>www.youtube.com/ketodietchannel</u>

<u>www.facebook.com/ketodietchannel</u>

❋ CONTENTS ❋

BASIC WAFFLE 10

SWEET WAFFLE 11

PLAIN x CHOCOOLATE WAFFLE 12

MAPLE WALNUT WAFFLE 14

COCONUT WAFFLE 16

PEANUT WAFFLE 18

AVOCADO CHOCOLATE WAFFLE 20

PLAIN x CHOCOLATE WAFFLE CAKE WITH CHOCOLATE BUTTER CREAM 22

TIRAMISU WAFFLE 24

WAFFLE CHOCOLATE HEAVEN 26

WAFFLE "CREAM PUFFS" WITH CUSTARD FILLING 28

WAFFLE "CREAM PUFFS" WITH CHOCOLATE CUSTARD FILLING 30

LEMON WAFFLE DOME CAKE 32

CREATIVE KETO MINI WAFFLES

CINNAMON WAFFLE SKEWERS 34

LEMON COCONUT WAFFLE CAKE 36

TIRAMISU WAFFLE CUPS 38

PLAIN x CHOCOLATE CREAM WAFFLE CUPS 40

WALNUT COFFEE WAFFLE CAKE WITH COFFEE BUTTER CREAM 42

CHOCOLATE DIPPED PEANUT BUTTER SANDWICH WAFFLE 44

"CREAM CHEESE DANISH" WAFFLE 46

SESAME WAFFLE 48

NACHO CHEESE WAFFLE 50

KEEMA CURRY WAFFLE 52

SALMON AVOCADO WAFFLE 54

GARLIC SHRIMP WAFFLE 56

AVOCADO WAFFLE 58

CREATIVE KETO MINI WAFFLES

What's inside the author's first cookbook
'CREATIVE KETO KITCHEN'

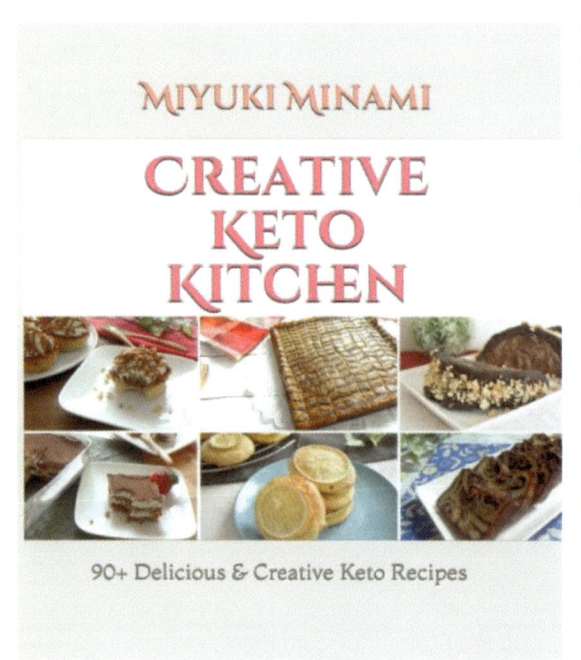

Recipe Index

- VANILLA CUSTARD BLUEBERRY MUFFINS 4
- CREAMY LEMON CURD RASPBERRY MUFFINS 6
- TWO-TONE CINNAMON DONUTS 8
- COCONUT COOKIES 10
- CINNAMON CHOCOLATE COCONUT FLOUR COOKIES 11
- LEMON CREAM CHEESE COOKIES 12
- LINGOTS AU CHOCOLAT 14
- ALMOND BUTTER BROWNIES 17
- CARAMEL SWIRL POUND CAKE 18
- CHOCOLATE & CARAMEL MOUSSE CAKE WITH COFFEE CARAMEL GLAZE 20
- TIRAMISU 23
- NO-BAKE PEANUT BUTTER CHOCOLATE ZEBRA CHEESECAKE 26
- COCONUT FLOUR VANILLA LAYER CAKE WITH BLUEBERRY FILLING 28
- THREE LAYER RASPBERRY CHEESECAKE MOUSSE TERRINE 30
- TRICOLOUR BUNDT CAKE (VANILLA, CHOCOLATE & CINNAMON) 32
- CARAMEL CHEESECAKE BARS 34
- ZEBRA CAKE 36
- CHOCOLATE TERRINE 38
- NO-BAKE CHEESECAKE WITH LEMON CURD FILLING 40
- CINNAMON BUNDT CAKE 42
- CHOCOLATE CHIP BROWNIE TOWER 44
- NO CRUST BAKED CHEESECAKE WITH BLUEBERRY COMPOTE 46
- DOUBLE CHOCOLATE LAYER CAKE 48
- RASPBERRY JELLY DOUBLE CHOCOLATE CHEESECAKE 50
- FLOURLESS PEANUT BUTTER CHOCOLATE CAKE 52
- LEMON JELLO CHEESECAKE 54
- CHOCOLATE BUTTERCREAM MERINGUE TOWER CAKE 56
- SOUFFLE CUSTARD PIE 58
- ALMOND BUTTER CHOCOLATE PIE 60
- VANILLA CUSTARD CHOCOLATE TARTLETS 62
- BUTTERY ALMOND TARTLETS 64
- PEANUT BUTTER CHOCOLATE MOUSSE TART 66
- CHOCOLATE ÉCLAIR CUPS WITH CARAMEL SAUCE 68
- NO-CHURN AVOCADO STRAWBERRY PROTEIN ICE CREAM 71
- CHOCOLATE DIPPED ICE CREAM TACOS (HOMEMADE CHOCO TACO) 72
- AVOCADO BERRY COCONUT CREAM POPSICLES 75
- NO-CHURN PEANUT BUTTER ICE CREAM 76
- TIRAMISU POPSICLES 78
- FROZEN PUMPKIN BITES 80
- MERINGUE COOKIE PEANUT BUTTER CHOCOLATE BARS 82
- MELT-IN-YOUR-MOUTH CHOCOLATE FUDGE 84
- COFFEE JELLY 85
- STRAWBERRY & YOGURT MOUSSE 86

viii

CREATIVE KETO MINI WAFFLES

Creative Keto Kitchen

- STRAWBERRY-STUFFED NO-BAKE CHOCOLATE CHEESECAKE BITES 88
- PEANUT BUTTER MASCARPONE JARS 90
- PANNA COTTA WITH BERRY JELLY 92
- MAGIC COFFEE MOUSSE 94
- MAPLE NUT BRIE 96
- LEMON CHEESECAKE SMOOTHIE 97
- AVOCADO CHOCOLATE SMOOTHIE 98
- SUPER-EASY KETO BREAD 99
- CREAM CHEESE DANISH 100
- CHEESY COCONUT FLOUR BISCUITS 103
- CURRY PUFFS 104
- CHOCOLATE BABKA 106
- CINNAMON BABKA WITH CINNAMON GLAZE 108
- FRENCH SAVORY CAKE (CAKE SALE) 111
- HAM, CREAM CHEESE & NUTS PULL-APART RING 112
- CHOCOLATE CINNAMON PULL-APART BREAD 114
- PEANUT BUTTER STUFFED SKILLET ROLLS WITH CHOCOLATE DIPPING SAUCE 116
- CHEESEBURGER STUFFED BAGUETTE 118
- HAM & EGG BUNS 120
- GARLIC SHRIMP AVOCADO BREAD 122
- BERRY TWIST BUNS 124
- SALMON AVOCADO CROQUE CAKE 126

Creative Keto Kitchen

- ZUCCHINI & HAM PASTRY ROSES 128
- CHOCOLATE CREAM HORNS 130
- BACON PAIN d'EPI 132
- CHEESY WEAVE 134
- SOUFFLE QUICHE 136
- BACON & CHEESE WRAPPED PORK BELLY 138
- CURRIED EGG ZUCCHINI BOATS 140
- PORK BURGER WRAPPED OKRA 141
- EGG, BACON & CHEESE STUFFED MEATLOAF 142
- CHICKEN CRUST HAM & BROCCOLI PIE 144
- PAN-FRIED BACON WRAPPED ZUCCHINI SKEWERS 146
- CHEESY AVOCADO STUFFED CHICKEN BURGERS 148
- DAIKON RADISH POTSTICKERS (JAPANESE GYOZA) 150
- BACON WRAPPED BROCCOLI STUFFED PORK CHOPS 152
- CABBAGE WRAPPED BRIE STUFFED MEATBALL 154
- EGGS IN PORK BURGERS 156
- JAPANESE RAMEN 158
- CHICKEN OKRA TOMATO SOUP 160
- JAPANESE CHICKEN CURRY 162
- BACON & NAPA CABBAGE HOT POT WITH BRIE 164
- SUSHI DONUTS 166
- CURRIED EGG & AVOCADO SALAD CHEESE CUPS 168

Creative Keto Kitchen

- CAULIFLOWER RICE ONIGIRAZU 170
- SALMON & AVOCADO POCKETS 173
- BRAIDED CUCUMBER SUSHI 174
- JAPANESE OMELETTE (TAMAGOYAKI) 176
- JAPANESE STYLE BLACK SESAME GREEN BEANS 178
- BACON WRAPPED AVOCADO STUFFED BRIE 179
- HOMEMADE PROTEIN CHIPS 180
- CINNAMON PROTEIN CHIPS 182
- HOMEMADE "DORITOS" 184

On Sale on Amazon!

BASIC WAFFLE

Prep Time 2 minute
Cook Time 10 minutes
Total Time 12 minutes
Servings 2 waffles

❋ Ingredients

- 1 Egg, Room Temp
- 1.5 oz (42 g) Shredded Mozzarella Cheese
- 2 tbsp Almond Flour
- 1 tbsp Heavy Cream
  (Omit if you want them crunchy)
- 1/2 tsp Aluminum Free Baking Powder

❋ Instructions

1. Preheat your mini waffle maker.
2. In a small mixing bowl, combine together all the ingredients except for the cheese.
3. When the waffle maker is ready, sprinkle 1/4 of the cheese and let melt. 
4. Pour 1/2 of the batter on top of the melted cheese and then sprinkle the same amount of cheese. Close the lid and cook 4 - 5 minutes. (Push down the lid of your waffle iron for several seconds while cooking.) 
5. Remove with tongs.
6. Repeat with the remaining cheese and batter.

❋ Recipe Notes

You can add garlic powder, or other seasonings of your choice. Also, you can use other kinds of cheese.

❋ Approximate Nutritional Values Per Serving:

Calories 164 kcal, Protein 10.5 g, Fat 12.6 g, Carbohydrate 2.6 g, Fiber 0.8 g, Sugar 0.8 g

SWEET WAFFLE

Prep Time 2 minute
Cook Time 10 minutes
Total Time 12 minutes
Servings 2 waffles

❋ Ingredients
- 1 Egg, Room Temp
- 1 oz (28 g) Cream Cheese, Softened
- 2 tbsp Almond Flour
- 1 tbsp Heavy Cream
- 1/4 tsp (or less) Stevia Powder
- 1/2 tsp Vanilla Extract
- 1/2 tsp Aluminum Free Baking Powder

❋ Instructions
1. Preheat your mini waffle maker.
2. In a blender, combine all the ingredients well.
3. When the waffle maker is ready, pour 1/2 of the batter.
4. Close the lid and cook 4 – 5 minutes. (Push down the lid of your waffle iron for several seconds while cooking.) Then remove with tongs.
5. Repeat with the remaining batter.

❋ Recipe Notes
You can add cocoa powder, chocolate chips, ground cinnamon, etc. Also, you can use shredded MOZZARELLA cheese instead of cream cheese.

❋ Approximate Nutritional Values Per Serving:
Calories 160 kcal, Protein 6.1 g, Fat 14.2 g, Carbohydrate 2.3 g, Fiber 0.8 g, Sugar 0.9 g

PLAIN & CHOCOOLATE WAFFLE

Prep Time 5 minute
Cook Time 16 minutes
Total Time 21 minutes
Servings 4 waffles

✱ **Ingredients**

With Regular Cocoa (Makes 4 waffles)
- 1 Egg, Room Temp
- 1.5 Egg Whites, Room Temp
- 2 oz (56 g) Cream Cheese, Softened
- 1 tbsp Coconut Flour
- 2 tbsp Heavy Cream
- 1/4 tsp Stevia Powder
- 1 tsp Vanilla Extract
- 1/2 tsp Aluminum Free Baking Powder
- A Pinch Ground Cinnamon
- 1 tbsp Unsweetened Cocoa Powder

With Dark Cocoa (Makes 4 waffles)
- 2 Eggs, Room Temp
- 2 oz (56 g) Cream Cheese, Softened
- 1 tbsp Coconut Flour
- 2 tbsp Heavy Cream
- 1/4 tsp Stevia Powder
- 1 tsp Vanilla Extract
- 1/2 tsp Aluminum Free Baking Powder
- A Pinch Ground Cinnamon
- 2 tsp Unsweetened Cocoa Powder
- 1tsp Black Cocoa Powder

✽ Instructions

1. Cut out aluminum foil into an about 5 inch / 12.5 cm square. Roll up tightly to make a 5 inch / 12.5 cm long stick. Repeat to make one more.

2. Place the aluminum foil sticks on the waffle maker plate, making a cross. Fold one end of each stick as a handle. Then, remove.

3. Preheat your mini waffle maker.
4. In a blender, combine well all the ingredients except for the cocoa powder.
5. Transfer 1/2 of the batter into a bowl. Add the cocoa powder into the blender and blend. (Now you have two colors of batter.)
6. When the waffle maker is ready, place the aluminum foil sticks on the waffle maker plate, making a cross. Spoon about 2 teaspoons of plain batter and then 2 teaspoons of chocolate batter in each section. (Each batter may flow into the other sections. Feel free to take time and move it back even when it starts to get solid.)

7. Remove the sticks carefully. Add more batter here if necessary.

8. Close the lid and cook 3 - 4 minutes. (It depends on how long it took you to arrange each batter on the hot plate.) Then remove with tongs.
9. Repeat with the remaining batter.
10. Serve with desired toppings! (See pages 22 - 23, 38 - 39, and 40 - 41 for recipe ideas.)

✽ Recipe Notes

Impress your family and friends! You can enjoy two flavors in one waffle.

The color and flavor won't be so intense with regular cocoa powder. See the picture below.

✽ Approximate Nutritional Values Per Serving:

- **With Regular Cocoa**

  Calories 110 kcal, Protein 4.6 g, Fat 9.2 g, Carbohydrate 2.2 g, Fiber 1.0 g, Sugar 1.0 g

- **With Dark Cocoa**

  Calories 124 kcal, Protein 5.0 g, Fat 10.6 g, Carbohydrate 2.2 g, Fiber 1.0 g, Sugar 1.0 g

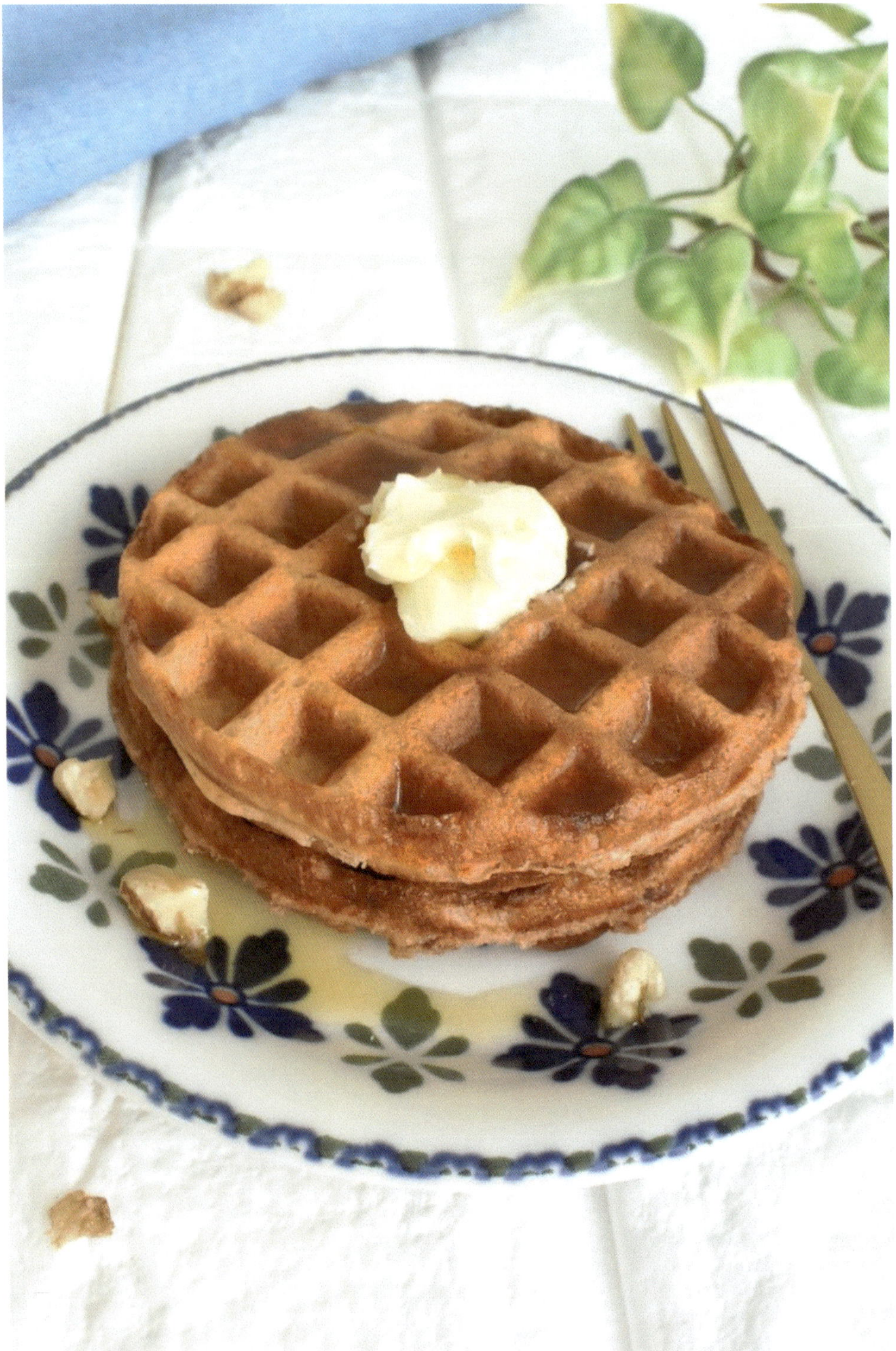

MAPLE WALNUT WAFFLE

Prep Time 5 minute
Cook Time 10 minutes
Total Time 15 minutes
Servings 2 waffles

✽ Ingredients

- 1 Egg, Room Temp
- 1 oz (28 g) Cream Cheese, Softened
- 1 tbsp Heavy Cream
- 1.5 tsp Sugar Free Maple Syrup
- 1/4 tsp Aluminum Free Baking Powder
- A Pinch Stevia Powder
- A Pinch Ground Cinnamon
- 1 oz (28 g) Walnuts

✽ Instructions

1. Chop 1/2 of the walnuts into tiny pieces.
2. Preheat your mini waffle maker.
3. In a blender, ground the remaining walnuts. Then, add all the other ingredients except for the chopped walnuts and blend well. Add the chopped walnuts and stir lightly.
4. When the waffle maker is ready, pour 1/2 of the batter.
5. Close the lid and cook 5 minutes. (Push down the lid of your waffle iron for several seconds while cooking.) Then, remove with tongs.
6. Repeat with the remaining batter.
7. Serve with sugar free maple syrup and butter!

✽ Recipe Notes
Add some maple extract if desired.

✽ Approximate Nutritional Values Per Serving:
Calories 206 kcal, Protein 6.4 g, Fat 19.6 g, Carbohydrate 2.3 g, Fiber 1.0 g, Sugar 1.2 g

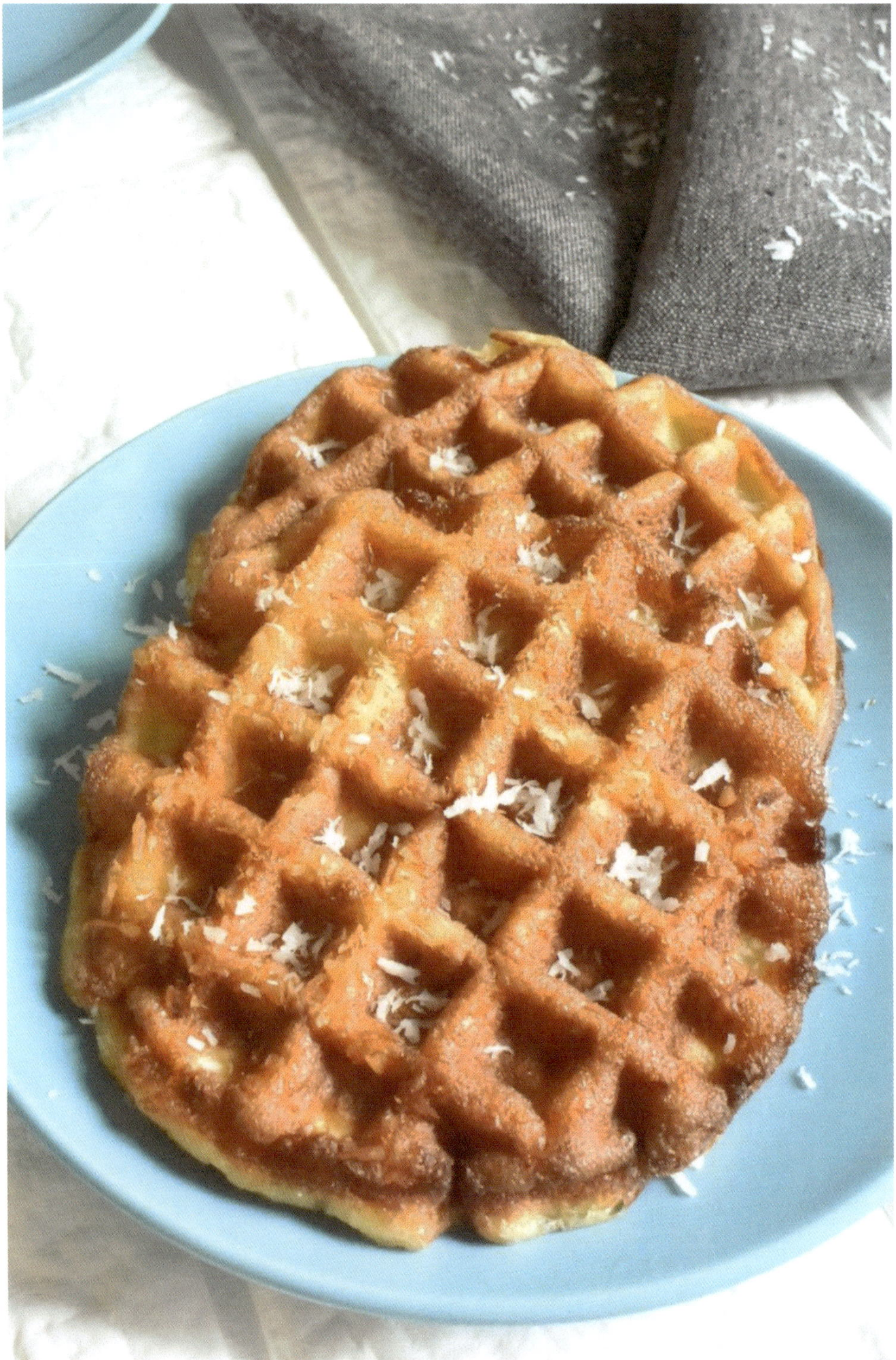

COCONUT WAFFLE

Prep Time 3 minute
Cook Time 10 minutes
Total Time 13 minutes
Servings 2 waffles

✱ Ingredients
- 1 Egg, Room Temp
- 1 oz (28 g) Cream Cheese, Softened
- 1 tbsp Unsweetened Shredded Coconut
- 1 tsp Coconut Flour
- 2 tsp Melted Coconut Oil (About 0.21 oz / 6 g)
- 1 tsp Heavy Cream
- 1/2 tsp Vanilla Extract
- 1/4 tsp Aluminum Free Baking Powder
- A Pinch Stevia Powder

✱ Instructions
1. Preheat your mini waffle maker.
2. In a blender, combine well all the ingredients.
3. When the waffle maker is ready, pour 1/2 of the batter.
4. Close the lid and cook 4 – 5 minutes. Then remove with tongs.
5. Repeat with the remaining batter.

✱ Recipe Notes
Add some coconut extract if desired.

✱ Approximate Nutritional Values Per Serving:
Calories 145 kcal, Protein 4.6 g, Fat 13.2 g, Carbohydrate 1.8 g, Fiber 0.8 g, Sugar 0.7 g

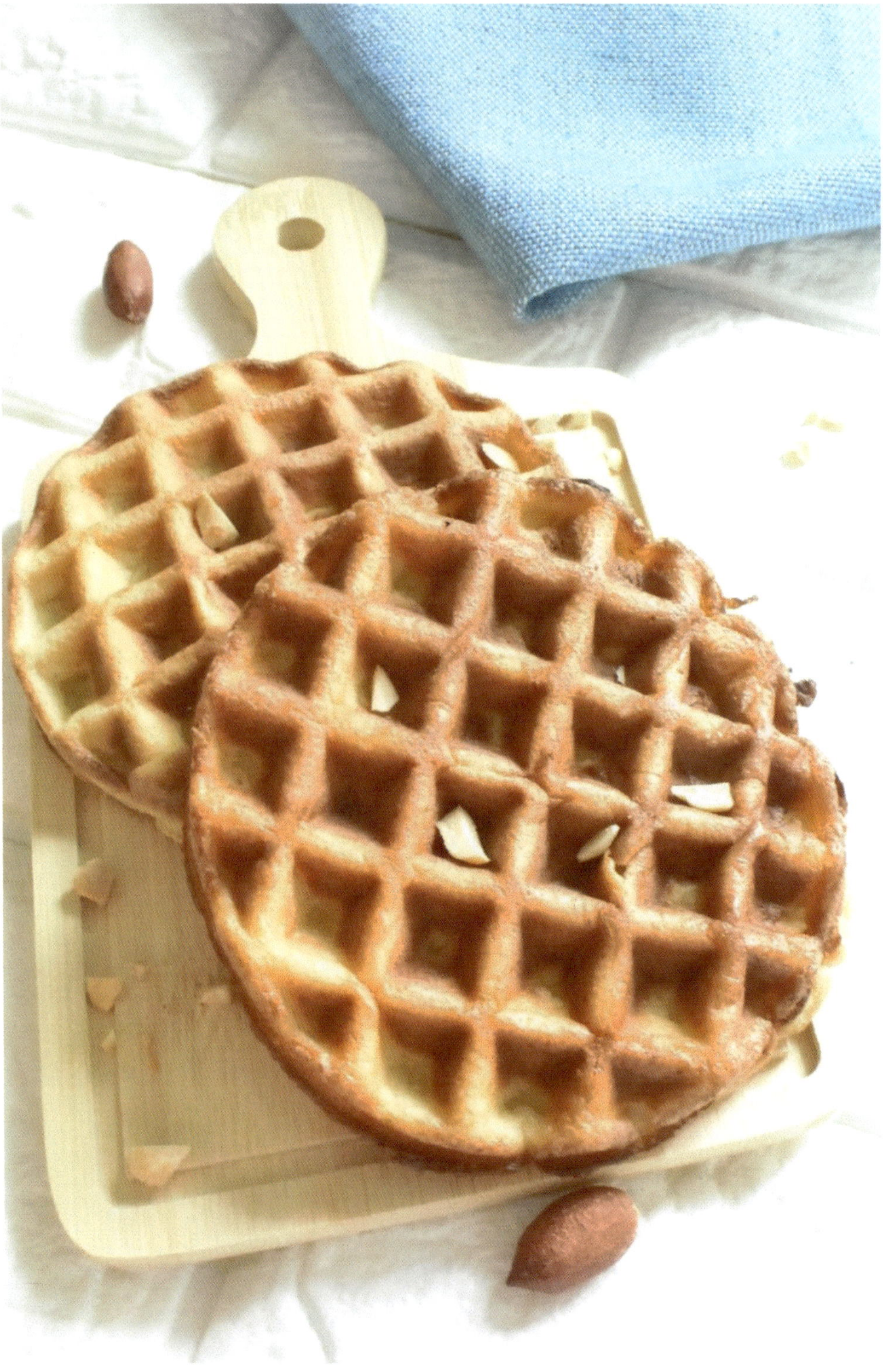

PEANUT WAFFLE

Prep Time 3 minute
Cook Time 10 minutes
Total Time 13 minutes
Servings 2 waffles

✽ Ingredients
- 1 Egg, Room Temp
- 1 oz (28 g) Cream Cheese, Softened
- 0.75 oz (21 g) Toasted Peanuts
- 1 tbsp Heavy Cream
- 1/2 tsp Vanilla Extract
- A Pinch Aluminum Free Baking Powder
- A Pinch Stevia Powder

✽ Instructions
1. Preheat your mini waffle maker.
2. In a blender, ground the peanuts. Then, add all the other ingredients and blend well.
3. When the waffle maker is ready, pour 1/2 of the batter.
4. Close the lid and cook 4 minutes. Then, remove with tongs.
5. Repeat with the remaining batter.

✽ **Approximate Nutritional Values Per Serving:**
Calories 174 kcal, Protein 6.5 g, Fat 15.5 g, Carbohydrate 2.5 g, Fiber 0.6 g, Sugar 0.9 g

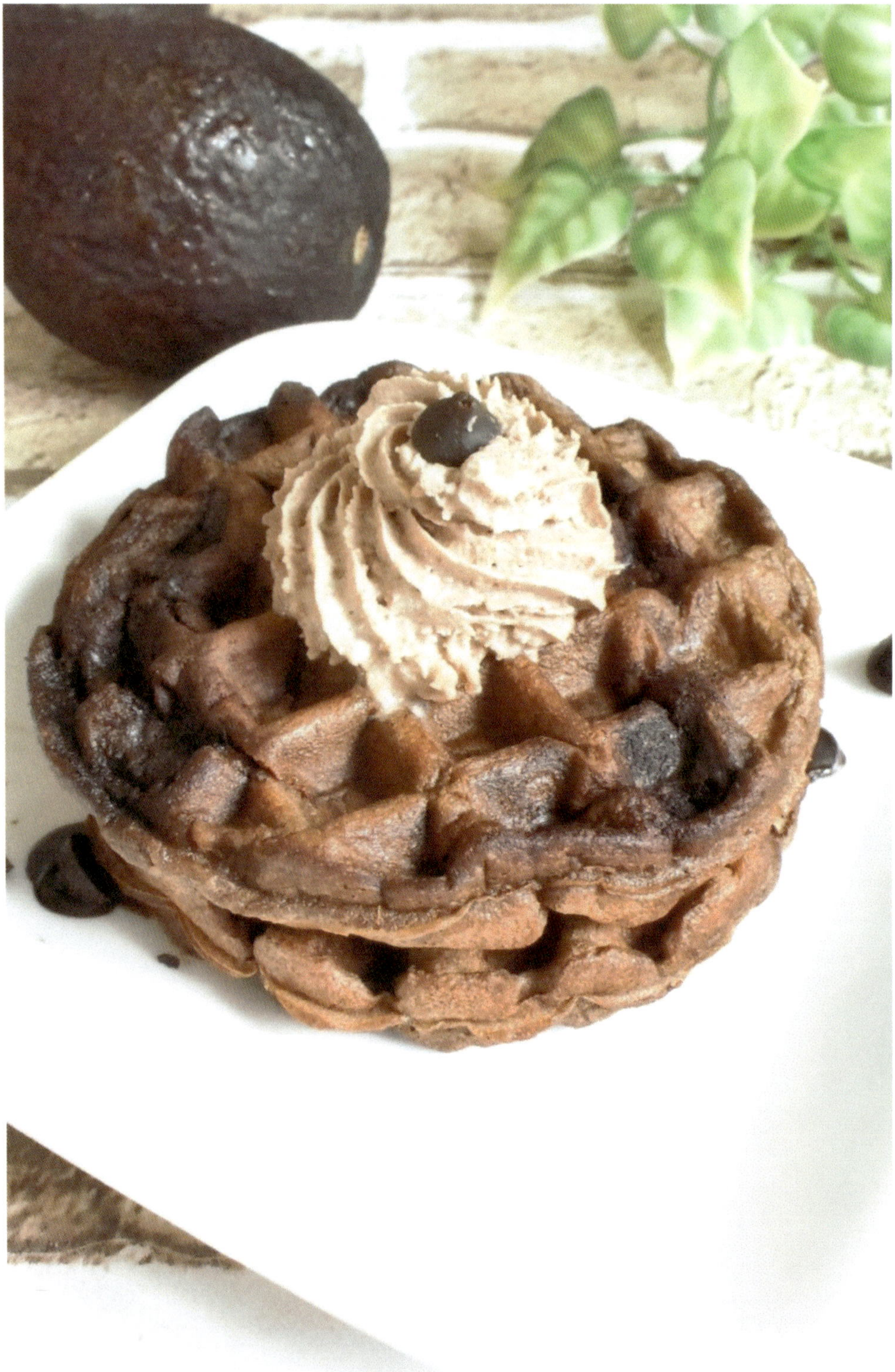

AVOCADO CHOCOLATE WAFFLE

❋ Approximate Nutritional Values Per Serving:
Calories 156 kcal, Protein 6.0 g, Fat 13.3 g, Carbohydrate 4.9 g, Fiber 3.0 g, Sugar 1.5 g

Prep Time 3 minute
Cook Time 8 minutes
Total Time 11 minutes
Servings 2 waffles

❋ Ingredients

- 1 Egg, Room Temp
- 1/4 Ripe Avocado
- 1 oz (28 g) Cream Cheese, Softened
- 1.5 tbsp Unsweetened Cocoa Powder
- 1 tbsp Coconut Flour
- 2 tbsp Heavy Cream
- 1 tsp Avocado Oil
- 1 tsp Vanilla Extract
- 1/4 tsp Aluminum Free Baking Powder
- 1/4 tsp Stevia Powder
- 1/4 tsp Ground Cinnamon
- A Pinch Sea Salt
- 1 tbsp Sugar Free Chocolate Chips (About 0.35 oz / 10 g)

❋ Instructions

1. Preheat your mini waffle maker.
2. In a blender, blend well all the ingredients except for the chocolate chips. (The batter would be very thick.)
3. When the waffle maker is ready, spoon 1/2 of the batter. Sprinkle 1/2 of the chocolate chips.
4. Close the lid and cook 4 minutes. Then, remove with tongs.
5. Repeat with the remaining batter and chocolate chips.
6. Enjoy with whipped cream!

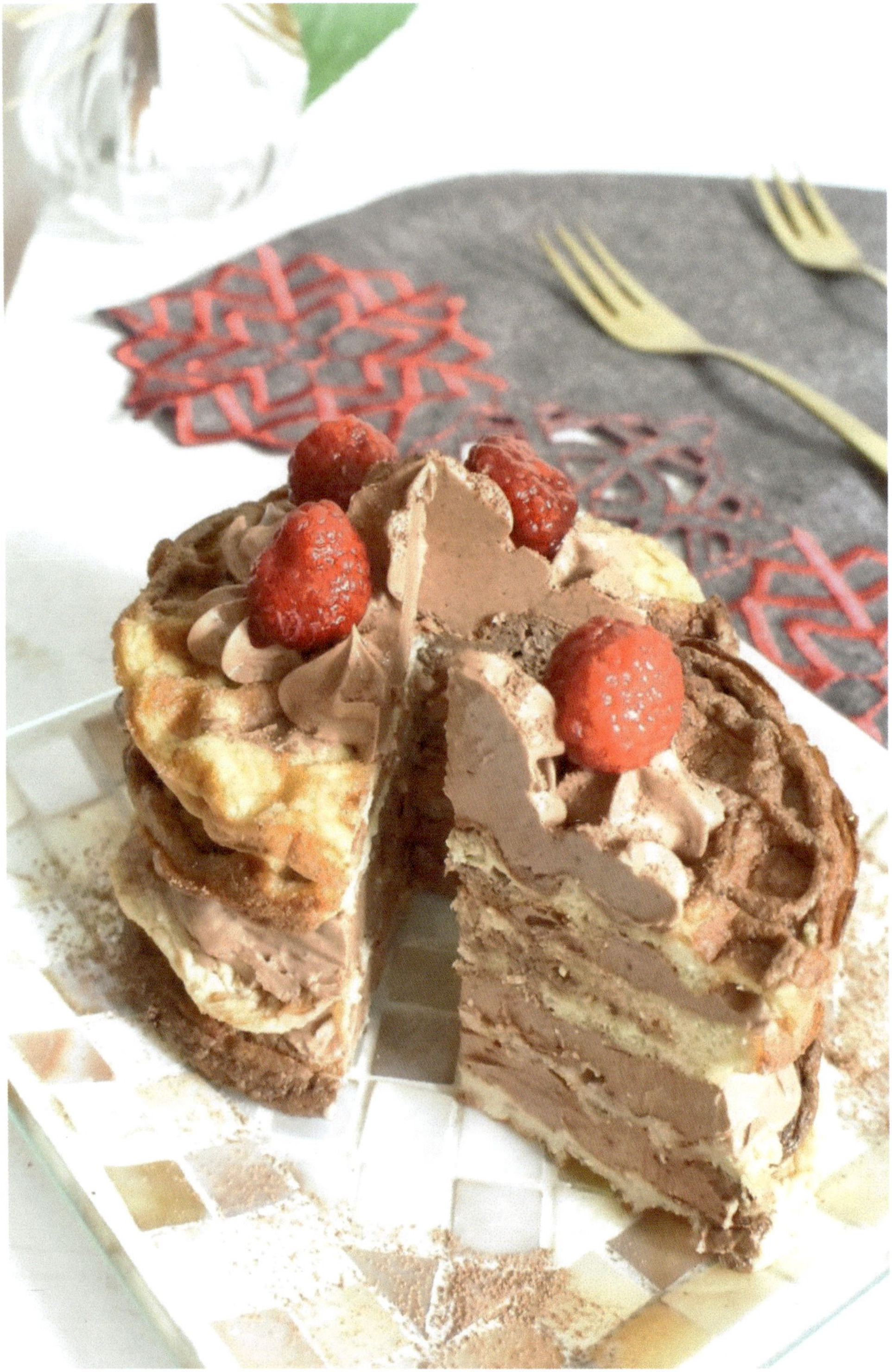

PLAIN x CHOCOLATE WAFFLE CAKE WITH CHOCOLATE BUTTER CREAM

Total Time 10 minutes (+ Chilling Time)
Servings 4 slices

❈ Ingredients

Waffles
- 4 Plain x Chocolate Waffles (Pages 12 - 13)

Chocolate Butter Cream
- 3 oz (85 g) Unsalted Butter, Softened
- 1/2 tbsp Stevia Powder
- 2 tbsp Unsweetened Cocoa Powder
- 1 tbsp Heavy Cream
- 2 tsp Vanilla Extract

❈ Instructions

Chocolate Butter Cream
1. Beat the butter and stevia powder with an electric mixer until pale and fluffy. Scrape down the sides of the bowl as necessary.
2. Add the cocoa, heavy cream, and vanilla. Beat until combined.

Assembly
1. Spread 1/4 of the chocolate butter cream on top of a waffle. Top with a second waffle and then spread the chocolate butter cream. Repeat with the remaining waffles and chocolate butter cream.
2. Serve immediately or chill until the chocolate butter cream is set to your liking.

❈ Recipe Notes

Bring to room temperature before serving after long refrigeration.

You can of course use simple chocolate waffles (Pages 26 - 27). The waffles in the pictures shown here are made with Regular Cocoa Powder, not Black Cocoa Powder.

❈ Approximate Nutritional Values Per Serving:

Calories 309 kcal, Protein 5.9 g, Fat 30.4 g, Carbohydrate 4.0 g, Fiber 1.9 g, Sugar 1.9 g

CREATIVE KETO MINI WAFFLES

TIRAMISU WAFFLE

Prep Time 10 minutes
Cook Time 20 minutes
Total Time 30 minutes (+ Chilling Time)
Servings 4 slices

✽ **Ingredients**

Waffles
- 2 Eggs, Room Temp
- 2 oz (56 g) Cream Cheese, Softened
- 1 tbsp Coconut Flour
- 1 tbsp Heavy Cream
- 1 tsp Vanilla Extract
- 1/2 tsp Aluminum Free Baking Powder
- 1/2 tsp Ground Cinnamon
- 1/4 tsp Stevia Powder

Coffee Syrup
- 4 tbsp Strong Coffee, Room Temp
- 5 drops Liquid Stevia

Filling
- 3 oz (85 g) Mascarpone Cheese, Room Temp
- 1 oz (28 g) Cream Cheese, Room Temp
- 1/4 cup (60 cc) Heavy Cream
- 2 tsp Vanilla Extract
- 1/4 tsp Stevia Powder

To Dust
- 1/2 tsp Unsweetened Cocoa Powder

✽ **Instructions**

Waffles (Makes 4 waffles)
1. Preheat your mini waffle maker.
2. In a blender, combine well all the ingredients.
3. When the waffle maker is ready, pour 1/4 of the batter.
4. Close the lid and cook 4 - 5 minutes. (Push down the lid of your waffle iron for several seconds while cooking.) Then, remove with tongs.
5. Repeat with the remaining batter.

Coffee Syrup
1. In a small bowl, mix well the coffee and liquid stevia.

Filling
1. In a bowl, beat the heavy cream, vanilla, and stevia powder until stiff peaks form. Set aside.
2. In a separate bowl, cream the cream cheese and mascarpone with a hand mixer. Then, fold in the whipped cream.

Assembly
1. Spoon one tablespoon of the coffee syrup on a waffle. Then, spread 1/4 of the filling on top of the waffle. Top with a second waffle. Repeat with the remaining until you have 4 layers.
2. Generously dust with cocoa powder.
3. Refrigerate <u>overnight or longer</u>.

✽ **Recipe Notes**
Overnight refrigeration is recommended.

✽ **Approximate Nutritional Values Per Serving:**
Calories 283 kcal, Protein 7.3 g, Fat 26.7 g, Carbohydrate 3.3 g, Fiber 0.9 g, Sugar 1.9 g

WAFFLE CHOCOLATE HEAVEN

Prep Time 10 minutes
Cook Time 18 minutes
Total Time 28 minutes
Servings 4 slices

❋ Ingredients

Waffles
- 2 Eggs, Room Temp
- 2 oz (56 g) Cream Cheese, Softened
- 3 tbsp Unsweetened Cocoa Powder
- 2 tbsp Heavy Cream
- 1 tbsp Coconut Flour
- 2 tsp Vanilla Extract
- 1/2 tsp Aluminum Free Baking Powder
- 1/2 tsp Ground Cinnamon
- 1/4 tsp (or more) Stevia Powder
- A Pinch Sea Salt

Chocolate Sauce
- 1/3 cup + 1 tbsp (95 cc) Heavy Cream
- 1.5 oz (42 g) Unsweetened Baking Chocolate, Chopped
- 1.5 tsp Liquid Stevia
- 1.5 tsp Vanilla Extract

✱ Instructions

Waffles (Makes 4 waffles)
1. Preheat your mini waffle maker.
2. In a blender, combine well all the ingredients.
3. When the waffle maker is ready, spoon 1/4 of the batter.
4. Close the lid and cook 4 minutes. (Push down the lid of your waffle iron for several seconds while cooking.) Then, remove with tongs.
5. Repeat with the remaining batter.

Chocolate Sauce
1. In a saucepan, bring the heavy cream to a simmer over low heat.
2. Turn off the heat and add the chocolate. Leave a couple of minutes, and then stir until melted.
3. Add the liquid stevia and vanilla and stir well.

Assembly
1. Place one waffle on a plate. Spread about one tablespoon of the chocolate sauce.
2. Cut out the center of 2 waffles, using a 2 inch / 5 cm cookie cutter (or just using a knife). 
3. Place one of the waffles with a hole on the chocolate covered waffle on the plate. Spread about 2 teaspoons of the chocolate sauce. Place the other waffle with a hole on top. Then, place the cut-out waffle centers into the hole (or you can just eat these centers if you want...). Compress with the back of a spoon to make room for the chocolate sauce. Then spoon the chocolate sauce into the hole.  
4. Spread about 2 teaspoons of the chocolate sauce on the waffle with a hole, and then place the remaining whole waffle on top.
5. (Optional) Top with whipped cream, cocoa powder, chopped nuts, etc.
6. Drizzle the left over chocolate sauce.
7. Slice and enjoy!

✱ Recipe Notes

This is like a molten lava cake. The chocolate sauce will ooze out when sliced.
Refrigeration will make the chocolate sauce solid, so assemble right before serving.

✱ Approximate Nutritional Values Per Serving:
Calories 268 kcal, Protein 7.3 g, Fat 25.7 g, Carbohydrate 7.7 g, Fiber 3.5 g, Sugar 2.4 g

WAFFLE "CREAM PUFFS" WITH CUSTARD FILLING

Prep Time 15 minutes
Cook Time 23 minutes
Total Time 38 minutes (+ Chilling Time)
Servings 4

✽ Ingredients

Waffles
- 2 Eggs, Room Temp
- 2 oz (56 g) Cream Cheese, Softened
- 1 tbsp Coconut Flour
- 1 tbsp Heavy Cream
- 1 tsp Vanilla Extract
- 1/2 tsp Aluminum Free Baking Powder
- 1/2 tsp Ground Cinnamon
- 1/4 tsp Stevia Powder

Custard Filling
- 4 Egg Yolks
- 1 tbsp Stevia Powder
- 1/4 tsp Xanthan Gum
- 1 cup (240 cc) Heavy Cream
- 1 tbsp Vanilla Extract

To Dust
- 1/2 tsp Confectioners Swerve

✱ Instructions

Custard Filling

1. Whisk the egg yolks and stevia powder in a bowl until a pale yellow. Add the xanthan gum and whisk well.
2. Bring the heavy cream to almost a simmer in a saucepan. Add to the egg yolk mixture. QUICKLY whisk to combine, and then transfer the mixture to the saucepan.
3. Keep stirring the mixture with a spatula or whisk over low – medium heat. Don't stop! When it starts to thicken, stir 20 – 30 more seconds.
4. Turn off the heat and stir 20 – 30 more seconds. Add the vanilla and mix well.
5. Strain the custard cream through a fine mesh sieve to make it smooth. Place a piece of cling wrap over the custard. Stick the wrap to the custard by pressing lightly to prevent a film from forming on top of the custard.
6. Refrigerate for one hour or until cold.

Waffles (Makes 4 waffles)

1. While chilling the custard, preheat your mini waffle maker.
2. In a blender, combine well all the ingredients.
3. When the waffle maker is ready, pour 1/4 of the batter.
4. Close the lid and cook 4 – 5 minutes. (Push down the lid of your waffle iron for several seconds while cooking.) Then, remove with tongs.
5. Repeat with the remaining batter.
6. Let them cool completely.

Assembly

1. Remove the custard from the fridge. Remove the wrap carefully and transfer to a bowl. Cream the custard with a whisk. If too thick, add a little bit of heavy cream. Place in a piping bag.
2. Cut a pocket into each waffle by inserting a small sharp kitchen knife 1/4 of the circle rim slowly and carefully. Watch carefully as you go not to make big holes. (Tiny holes are inevitable.)
3. Pipe the custard into each pocket.
4. Dust with sweetener.
5. Serve immediately or chill for a couple hours. (Refrigeration makes them tastier.)

✱ Recipe Notes
Keep refrigerated. Eat within 2 – 3 days.

✱ Approximate Nutritional Values Per Serving:
Calories 390 kcal, Protein 9.1 g, Fat 37.7 g, Carbohydrate 3.2 g, Fiber 0.6 g, Sugar 2.4 g (Swerve is not counted as carbs as it doesn't affect blood sugar levels.)

WAFFLE "CREAM PUFFS" WITH CHOCOLATE CUSTARD FILLING

Prep Time 15 minutes
Cook Time 10 minutes
Total Time 25 minutes (+ Chilling Time)
Servings 2

✻ Ingredients

Waffles
- 1 Egg, Room Temp
- 1 oz (28 g) Cream Cheese, Softened
- 4 tsp Unsweetened Cocoa Powder
- 1/2 tbsp Coconut Flour
- 1.5 tbsp Heavy Cream
- 1 tsp Vanilla Extract
- 1/2 tsp Aluminum Free Baking Powder
- 1/4 tsp Ground Cinnamon
- 1/4 tsp Stevia Powder
- A Pinch Sea Salt

Chocolate Custard Filling
- 2 Egg Yolks
- 2 tsp Stevia Powder
- 1/8 tsp Xanthan Gum
- 1/2 cup (120 cc) Heavy Cream
- 2 tsp Vanilla Extract
- 0.63 oz (18 g) Unsweetened Baking Chocolate, Finely Chopped
- 1 - 3 tsp Heavy Cream (Adjust) (To be added after refrigeration)

✽ Instructions

Chocolate Custard Filling

1. Whisk the egg yolks and stevia powder in a bowl until a pale yellow. Add the xanthan gum and whisk well.
2. Bring the heavy cream to almost a simmer in a saucepan. Add to the egg yolk mixture. QUICKLY whisk to combine, and then transfer the mixture to the saucepan.
3. Keep stirring the mixture with a spatula or whisk over low – medium heat. Don't stop! When it starts to thicken, stir 20 – 30 more seconds.
4. Turn off the heat and stir 20 – 30 more seconds. Add the vanilla and mix well.
5. Strain the custard cream through a fine mesh sieve to make it smooth. Then, add the unsweetened chocolate while still warm and let sit for a couple of minutes. Stir well until melted and creamy.
6. Place a piece of cling wrap over the custard. Stick the wrap to the custard by pressing lightly to prevent a film from forming on top of the custard.
7. Refrigerate for one hour or until cold.

Waffles (Makes 2 waffles)

1. While chilling the custard, preheat your mini waffle maker.
2. In a blender, combine well all the ingredients.
3. When the waffle maker is ready, pour 1/2 of the batter.
4. Close the lid and cook 4 minutes. Then remove with tongs.
5. Repeat with the remaining batter.
6. Let them cool completely.

Assembly

1. Remove the custard from the fridge. Remove the wrap carefully and transfer to a bowl. Cream the custard with a whisk. Add 1 – 3 teaspoons of heavy cream to make it creamy. Place in a piping bag.
2. Cut a pocket into each waffle by inserting a small sharp kitchen knife 1/4 of the circle rim slowly and carefully. Watch carefully as you go not to make big holes. (Tiny holes are inevitable.)
3. Pipe the custard into each pocket.
4. Serve immediately.

✽ Recipe Notes

Keep refrigerated. Bring to room temperature before serving. Eat within 2 – 3 days.

✽ Approximate Nutritional Values Per Serving:

Calories 498 kcal, Protein 11.2 g, Fat 48.9 g, Carbohydrate 8.3 g, Fiber 3.0 g, Sugar 3.7 g

LEMON WAFFLE DOME CAKE

Prep Time 15 minutes
Cook Time 20 minutes
Total Time 35 minutes (+ Chilling Time)
Servings 4 slices

✲ Ingredients

Waffles

- 2 Eggs, Room Temp
- 2 oz (56 g) Cream Cheese, Softened
- 1 tbsp Coconut Flour
- 2 tsp Heavy Cream
- 2 tsp Lemon Juice
- 1/2 tsp Vanilla Extract
- 1/4 tsp Stevia Powder
- 1/4 tsp Baking Soda (Can omit)

Lemon Frosting

- 8 oz (227 g) Cream Cheese, Softened
- 2 oz (56 g) Unsalted Butter, Softened
- 1 tbsp Stevia Powder
- 1 tbsp Lemon Zest
- 1 tsp Lemon Juice
- 1/2 tsp Vanilla Extract

✲ Instructions

Waffles (Makes 4 waffles)

1. Preheat your mini waffle maker.
2. In a blender, combine well all the ingredients.
3. When the waffle maker is ready, pour 1/4 of the batter.

4. Close the lid and cook 4 – 5 minutes. Then remove with tongs.
5. Repeat with the remaining batter.
6. Let them cool completely.

Lemon Frosting
1. In a large bowl, beat all the ingredients.

Assembly
1. Cut TWO waffles in half. Leave the other two intact.
2. Line a small bowl with cling wrap. (The recipe quantities are perfect for <u>a bowl of inner circle diameter: 5 inch / 12.5 cm and height: 2.3 inch / 6 cm</u>. Please adjust the quantities to the size of your bowl.) 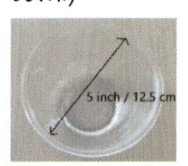
3. Place one whole waffle in the bottom of the bowl.
4. Line the sides of the bowl with the four semicircle waffles. 
5. Spoon in about half of the lemon frosting. Leave some room for the remaining whole waffle. 
6. Place the last waffle. 
7. Cover with cling wrap and chill for 30 minutes. (You can leave the rest of the lemon frosting at room temperature.)
8. Invert on a plate and then remove the bowl and cling wrap. 
9. Spread the remaining lemon frosting over the dome cake. Decorate if desired.
10. Chill for about 30 minutes.

✽ Recipe Notes
Bring to room temperature before serving after long refrigeration. This cake tastes better at room temperature because the frosting gets creamier and the waffles get softer.

✽ **Approximate Nutritional Values Per Serving:** Calories 405 kcal, Protein 9.2 g, Fat 38.7 g, Carbohydrate 2.8 g, Fiber 0.4 g, Sugar 2.2 g

CINNAMON WAFFLE SKEWERS

Prep Time 10 minutes
Cook Time 16 minutes
Total Time 26 minutes
Servings 3 skeweres

✽ Ingredients

Waffles
- 2 Eggs, Room Temp
- 2 oz (56 g) Cream Cheese, Softened
- 1 tbsp Coconut Flour
- 1 tbsp Heavy Cream
- 1 tsp Ground Cinnamon
- 1/2 tsp Vanilla Extract
- 1/2 tsp Aluminum Free Baking Powder (Can omit)
- 1/4 tsp Stevia Powder

Cinnamon Filling
- 2 oz (56 g) Unsalted Butter, Softened
- 1 tbsp Ground Cinnamon
- 1 tsp Stevia Powder

Cinnamon Glaze
- 1 oz (28 g) Confectioners Swerve (About 1/4 cup)
- 1 tsp Ground Cinnamon
- 1 tbsp + 1 tsp Water
- 1/2 tsp Vanilla Extract
- 3 drops Liquid Stevia

✤ **Instructions**

Waffles (Makes 4 waffles)
1. Preheat your mini waffle maker.
2. In a blender, combine well all the ingredients.
3. When the waffle maker is ready, pour 1/4 of the batter.
4. Close the lid and cook 4 minutes. Then remove with tongs.
5. Repeat with the remaining batter.
6. Let them cool.

Cinnamon Filling
1. In a bowl, beat the butter until fluffy.
2. Add the cinnamon and stevia powder. Beat to combine.

Cinnamon Glaze
1. Blend together all the ingredients.

Assembly
1. Flatten the waffles. 
2. Spread the cinnamon filling on the waffles.
3. Roll up a waffle lightly and thread onto three long skewers. Repeat with the remaining waffles.  
4. Cut the waffles between the skewers. 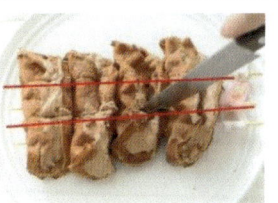
5. Drizzle the cinnamon glaze.
6. Serve immediately!

✤ **Recipe Notes**
Keep refrigerated. Bring to room temperature before serving.
If you don't like your glaze to get crystalized after refrigeration, make right before serving. You can cut each waffle roll-up into three and then skewer one by one, but that may get messier than my way.

✤ **Approximate Nutritional Values Per Serving:**
Calories 290 kcal, Protein 6.3 g, Fat 27.4 g, Carbohydrate 3.7 g, Fiber 2.0 g, Sugar 0.9 g (Swerve is not counted as carbs as it doesn't affect blood sugar levels.)

LEMON COCONUT WAFFLE CAKE

Prep Time 10 minutes
Cook Time 20 minutes
Total Time 30 minutes (+ Chilling Time)
Servings 4 slices

❈ Ingredients

Waffles
- 2 Eggs, Room Temp
- 2 oz (56 g) Cream Cheese, Softened
- 1 tbsp Unsweetened Shredded Coconut
- 2 tsp Coconut Flour
- 1 tbsp Heavy Cream
- 1 tbsp Melted Coconut Oil (0.5 oz / 14 g)
- 1 tsp Lemon Juice
- 1/2 tsp Vanilla Extract
- 1/4 tsp Stevia Powder
- 1/4 tsp Baking Soda (Can omit)

Lemon Curd
- 2 Eggs
- 2 Egg Yolks
- 1/2 cup (120 cc) Lemon Juice
- 2 tsp Stevia Powder
- 1/4 tsp Xanthan Gum
- 2 oz (56 g) Unsalted Butter

Topping
- 1 tbsp Unsweetened Shredded Coconut, Toasted

✽ Instructions

Lemon Curd
1. Whisk together the eggs, egg yolks, lemon juice and stevia powder in a saucepan.
2. Add the xanthan gum and whisk well to combine.
3. Add the butter and cook the mixture over low - medium heat, stirring frequently until thick. Remove from the heat.
4. Strain the lemon curd through a fine mesh sieve into a bowl.
5. Place a piece of cling wrap over the lemon curd. Stick the wrap to the lemon curd by pressing lightly.
6. Chill for one hour or until cold.

Waffles (Makes 4 waffles)
1. Preheat your mini waffle maker.
2. In a blender, combine all the ingredients well.
3. When the waffle maker is ready, pour 1/4 of the batter.
4. Close the lid and cook 3.5 - 4 minutes. Then remove with tongs.
5. Repeat with the remaining batter.
6. Let them cool completely.

Assembly
1. Spread 1/4 of the lemon curd on top of a waffle. Top with a second waffle and spread the lemon curd. Repeat with the remaining waffles and lemon curd.
2. Sprinkle the toasted shredded coconut on top.
3. Chill for about 30 minutes.

✽ Approximate Nutritional Values Per Serving:
Calories 345 kcal, Protein 9.6 g, Fat 31.7 g, Carbohydrate 4.6 g, Fiber 0.5 g, Sugar 3.5 g

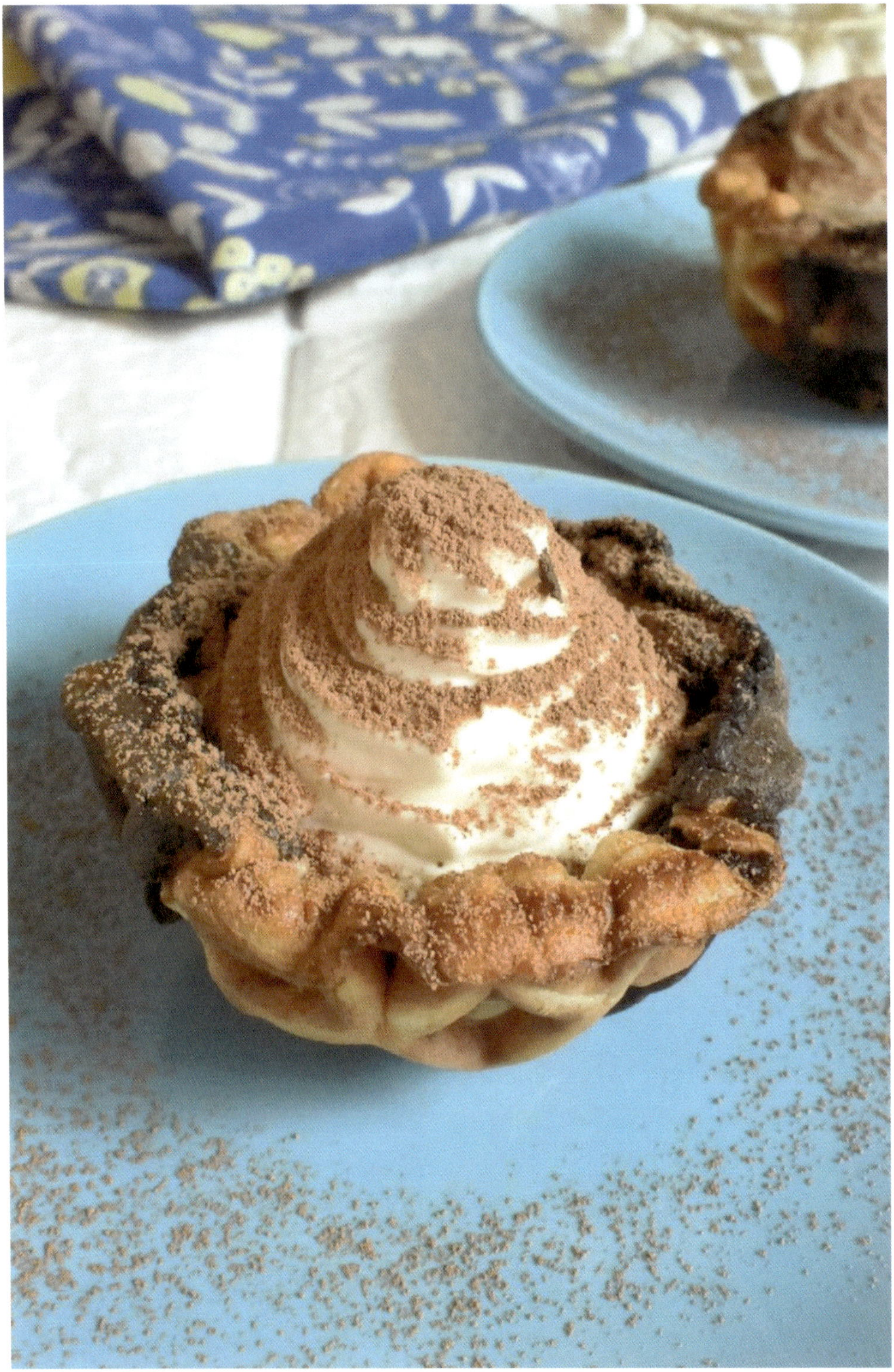

TIRAMISU WAFFLE CUPS

Total Time 5 minutes (+ Chilling Time)
Servings 2 cups

✻ Ingredients

Waffles
- 2 Plain x Chocolate Waffles (Pages 12 – 13)

Coffee Syrup
- 1 tbsp Strong Coffee, Room Temp
- 2 – 3 drops Liquid Stevia

Filling
- 1 oz (28 g) Mascarpone Cheese, Room Temp
- 1 oz (28 g) Cream Cheese, Room Temp
- 3 tbsp Heavy Cream
- 1.5 tsp Vanilla Extract
- 1/4 tsp Stevia Powder

To Dust
- 1/4 tsp Unsweetened Cocoa Powder

✻ Instructions

Waffles
1. Place the waffles into each cup of a muffin tin and shape into a cup. Set aside.

Coffee Syrup
1. In a small bowl, mix well the coffee and liquid stevia.

Filling
1. In a bowl, beat the heavy cream, vanilla, and stevia powder until stiff peaks form. Set aside.
2. In a separate bowl, cream the cream cheese and mascarpone with a hand mixer. Then, fold in the whipped cream.

Assembly
1. Spoon 1.5 teaspoons of the coffee syrup on the bottom (and sides) of each waffle cup. Let the waffles soak up.
2. Pipe or spoon the filling evenly into each cup.
3. Generously dust with cocoa powder.
4. Refrigerate in the muffin tin for at least 4 hours.

✻ Recipe Notes
You can use other sweet waffles of your choice.

✻ Approximate Nutritional Values Per Serving (With Black Cocoa Waffle):
Calories 314 kcal, Protein 7.7 g, Fat 30.0 g, Carbohydrate 3.7 g, Fiber 0.9 g, Sugar 2.4 g

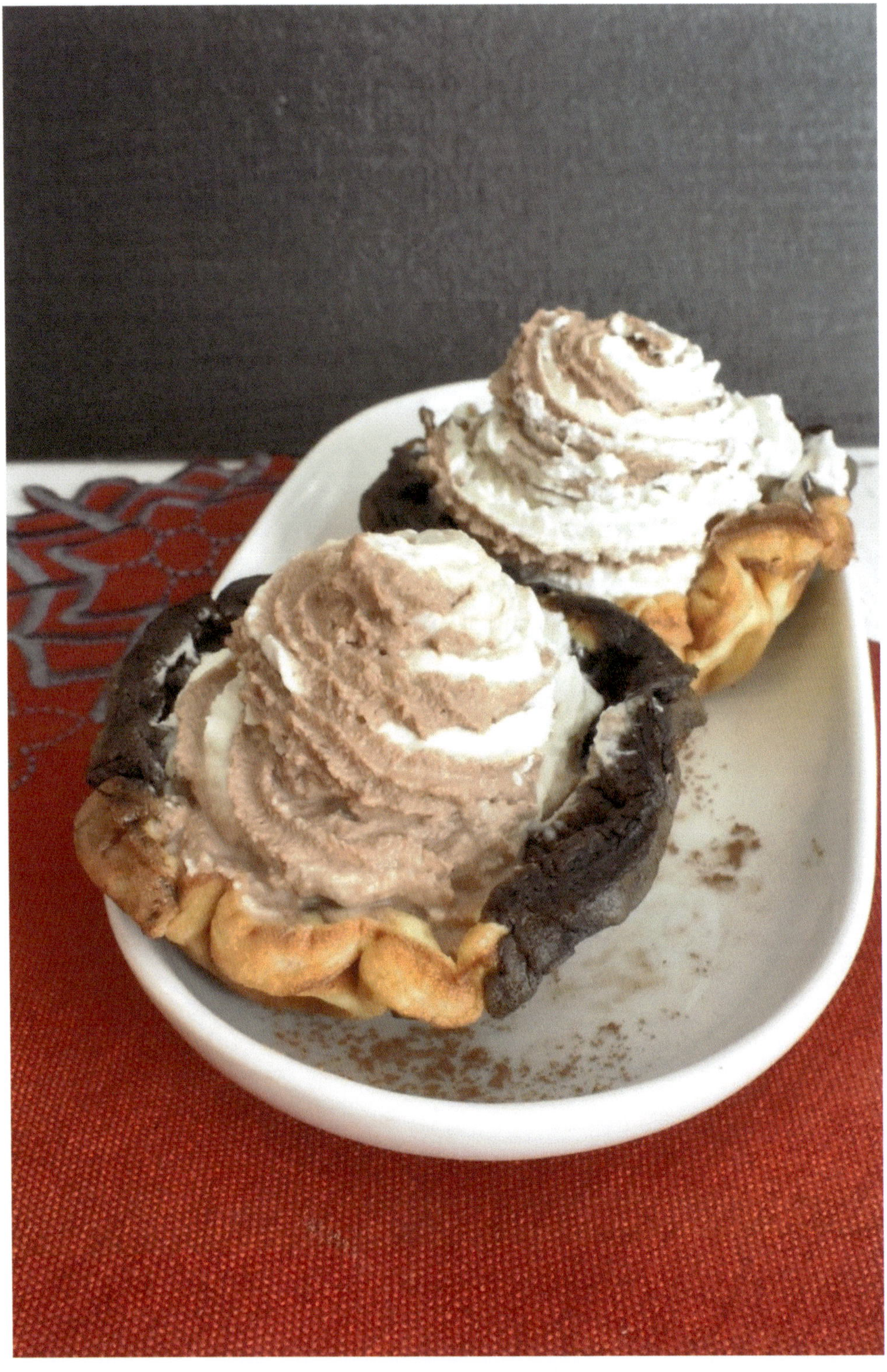

PLAIN x CHOCOLATE CREAM WAFFLE CUPS

Total Time 5 minutes
Servings 2 cups

✿ Ingredients

Waffles
- 2 Plain x Chocolate Waffles (Pages 12 – 13)

Plain Whipped Cream
- 3 tbsp (45 cc) Heavy Cream
- 1/2 tsp Stevia Powder
- 1/2 tsp Vanilla Extract

Chocolate Whipped Cream
- 3 tbsp (45 cc) Heavy Cream
- 1.5 tsp Unsweetened Cocoa Powder, Shifted
- 1/2 tsp Stevia Powder
- 1/2 tsp Vanilla Extract

✿ Instructions

Waffles
1. Place the waffles into each cup of a muffin tin while still warm and shape into a cup. Set aside to let completely cool.

Plain Whipped Cream
1. Beat all the ingreadients until stiff peaks form.

Chocolate Whipped Cream
1. Beat all the ingreadients until <u>medium</u> peaks form.

Assembly
1. Place both whipped cream next to each other in one piping bag.

2. Pipe into each cup and remove from the muffin tin.

✿ Recipe Notes

Enjoy the color alternating waffle cups and whipped cream! You can of course use other sweet waffles of your choice.

✿ Approximate Nutritional Values Per Serving (With Black Cocoa Waffle):

Calories 280 kcal, Protein 6.0 g, Fat 27.3 g, Carbohydrate 3.8 g, Fiber 1.1 g, Sugar 2.5 g

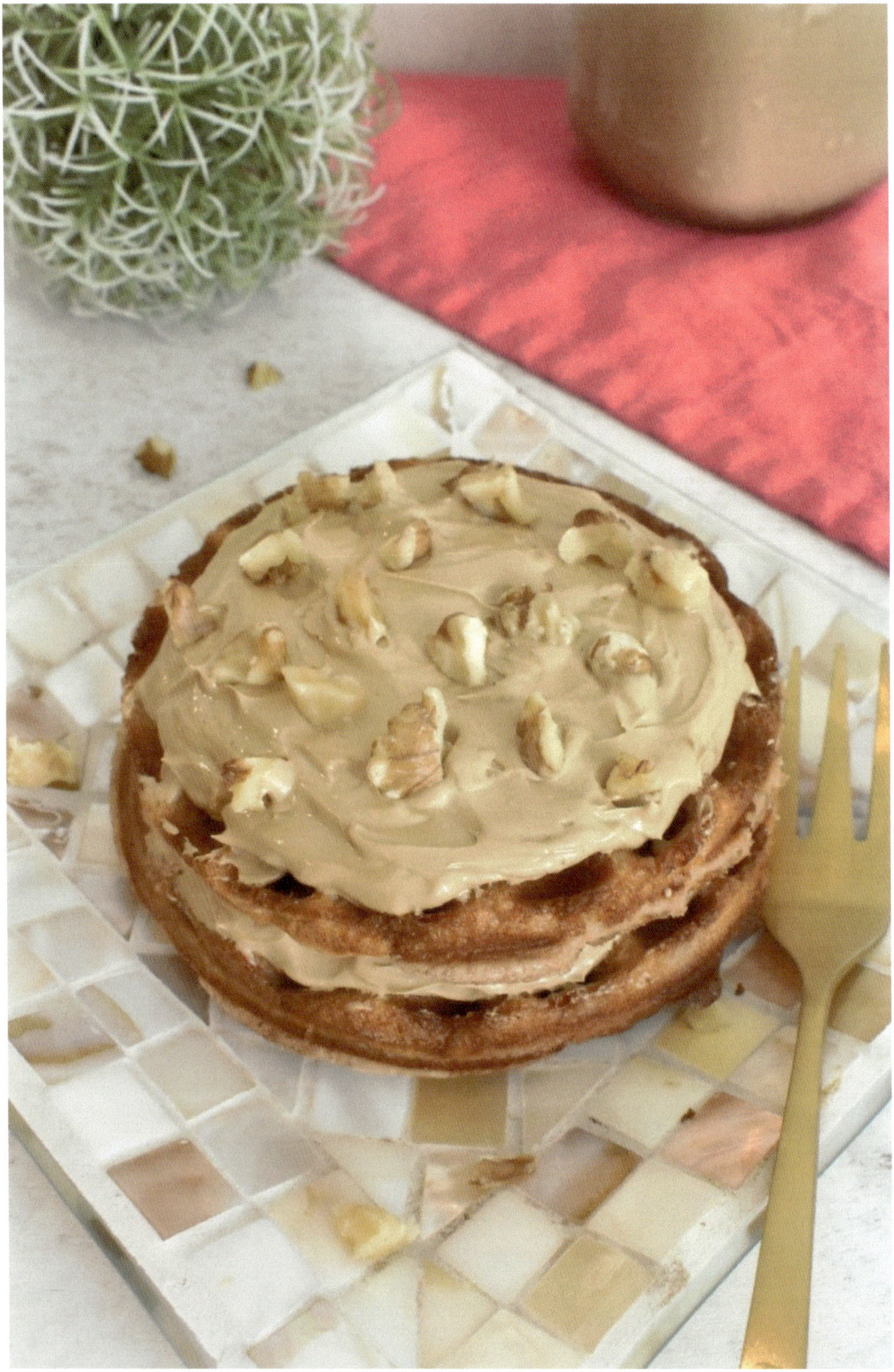

WALNUT COFFEE WAFFLE CAKE WITH COFFEE BUTTER CREAM

Prep Time 10 minute
Cook Time 10 minutes
Total Time 20 minutes
Servings 2 slices

❋ Ingredients

Waffles
- 1 Egg, Room Temp
- 1 oz (28 g) Cream Cheese, Softened
- 1 tbsp Heavy Cream
- 2 tsp Strong Coffee
- 1/4 tsp Aluminum Free Baking Powder
- A Pinch Stevia Powder
- A Pinch Ground Cinnamon
- 1 oz (28 g) Walnuts

Coffee Butter Cream
- 1.5 oz (42 g) Unsalted Butter, Softened
- 1 tsp Stevia Powder
- 1.5 tsp Instant Coffee Granules
- 1.5 tsp Boiling Water
- 1.5 tsp Heavy Cream

Topping
- 0.25 oz (7 g) Chopped Walnuts

❋ Instructions

Waffles (Makes 2 waffles)
1. Chop 1/2 of the walnuts into tiny pieces.
2. Preheat your mini waffle maker.
3. In a blender, ground the remaining walnuts. Then, add all the other ingredients except for the chopped walnuts and blend well. Add the chopped walnuts and stir lightly.
4. When the waffle maker is ready, pour 1/2 of the batter.
5. Close the lid and cook 5 minutes. (Push down the lid of your waffle iron for several seconds while cooking.) Then, remove with tongs.
6. Repeat with the remaining batter.

Coffee Butter Cream
1. In a small bowl, dissolve the coffee in the boiling water. Stir well. (It may take some time.) When dissolved, add the heavy cream and mix well.
2. Beat the butter and stevia powder with an electric mixer until pale and fluffy. Scrape down the sides of the bowl as necessary. Add the coffee mixture in 3 - 4 parts. Beat well to combine in each addition.

Assembly
1. Spread 1/2 of the coffee butter cream on top of a waffle. Top with the remaining waffle and then spread the remaining coffee butter cream.
2. Top with the walnuts.
3. Serve immediately or chill until the butter cream is set to your liking.

❋ Recipe Notes

Bring to room temperature before serving after long refrigeration.

❋ Approximate Nutritional Values Per Serving:

Calories 433 kcal, Protein 7.5 g, Fat 43.5 g, Carbohydrate 3.9 g, Fiber 1.2 g, Sugar 2.6 g

CREATIVE KETO MINI WAFFLES

CHOCOLATE DIPPED PEANUT BUTTER SANDWICH WAFFLE

Prep Time 10 minutes
Cook Time 2 minutes
Total Time 12 minutes (+ Chilling Time)
Servings 2

✱ Ingredients

Waffles
- 2 Peanut Waffles (Page 18 – 19)

Peanut Butter Filling
- 1 tbsp Unsweetened Peanut Butter, Room Temp
- 1.5 tbsp Unsalted Butter, Softened
- 1 tsp Cream Cheese, Softened
- 1/4 tsp Vanilla Extract
- A Pinch Stevia Powder

Chocolate Dip
- 0.24 oz (7 g) Coconut Oil
- 0.6 oz (17 g) Unsweetened Baking Chocolate, Finely Chopped
- 1/2 tsp Vanilla Extract
- 5 – 10 drops Liquid Stevia

Topping
- 2 tsp Crushed Salted Peanuts (About 0.17 oz / 5 g)

✱ Instructions

Peanut Butter Filling
1. In a bowl, beat the butter until fluffy.
2. Add the remaining ingredients and beat until well blended.

Chocolate Dip
1. Melt the coconut oil in a saucepan over low heat. Turn off the heat when half melted. (Or melt in a microwave.)
2. Add the unsweetened chocolate. Leave a couple minutes and then stir until melted.
3. Add the vanilla liquid stevia and mix well.

Assembly
1. Spread the peanut butter filling on a waffle. Top with the other waffle.
2. Roll the sandwich waffle in the melted chocolate. Sprinkle with the crushed peanuts.
3. Chill for 5 – 15 minutes until set.

✱ Approximate Nutritional Values Per Serving:
Calories 405 kcal, Protein 10.1 g, Fat 39.2 g, Carbohydrate 7.3 g, Fiber 2.7 g, Sugar 1.4 g

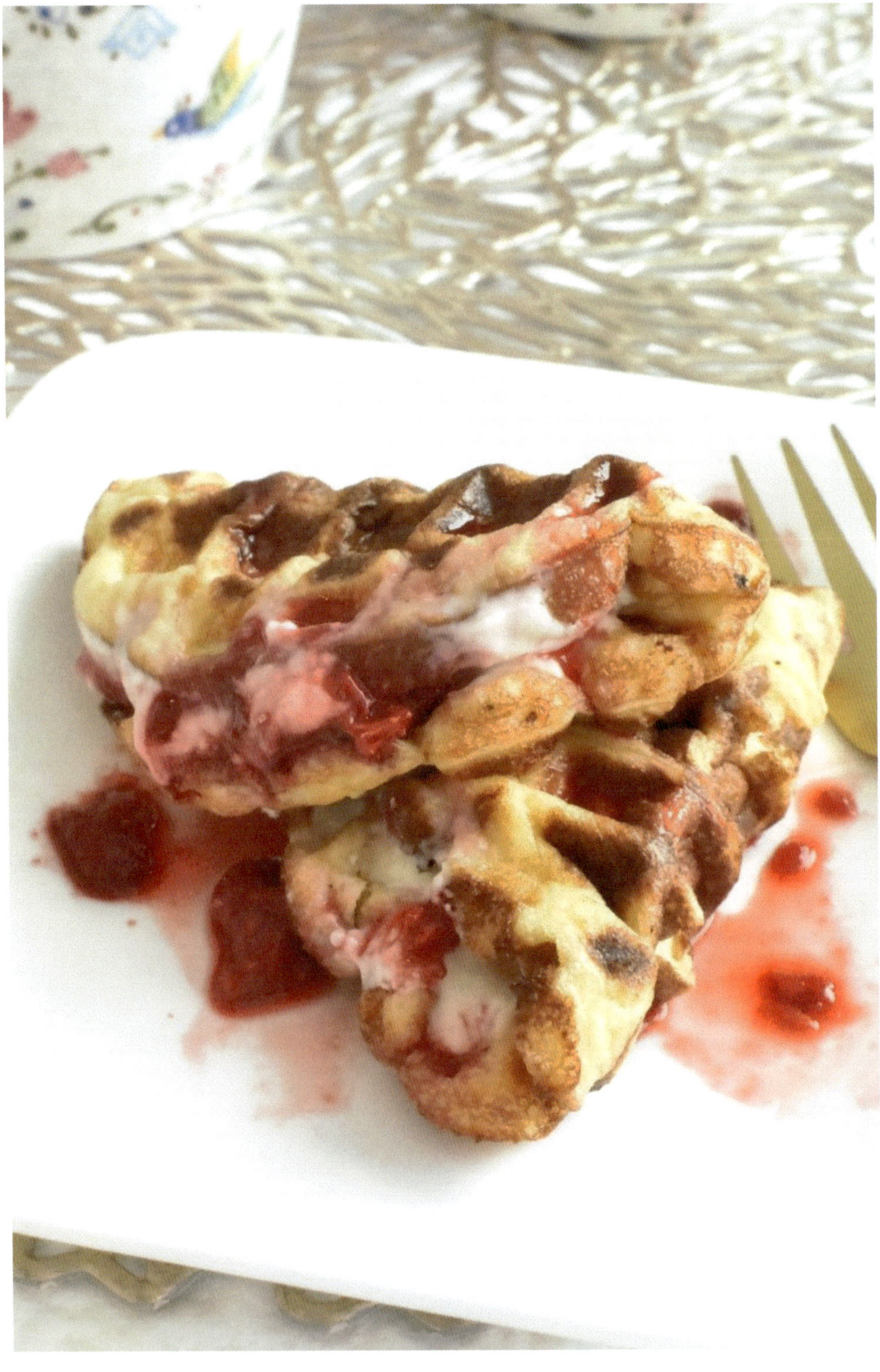

"CREAM CHEESE DANISH" WAFFLE

Prep Time 10 minutes
Cook Time 8 minutes
Total Time 18 minutes
Servings 2

❋ **Ingredients**

Waffles
- 1 Egg, Room Temp
- 1 oz (28 g) Cream Cheese, Softened
- 1.5 tsp Coconut Flour
- 1 tbsp Heavy Cream
- 1/2 tsp Vanilla Extract
- 1/4 tsp Aluminum Free Baking Powder
- 1/4 tsp (or less) Stevia Powder

Cream Cheese Filling
- 4 tsp Cream Cheese, Room Temp
- 1 tsp Heavy Cream
- 1/2 tsp Lemon Juice
- 1/4 tsp Vanilla Extract
- 5 drops Liquid Stevia
- 0.25 oz (7 g) Raspberries, Chopped

❋ **Instructions**

1. In a bowl, combine all the cream cheese filling ingredients except for the raspberries until creamy.
2. Preheat your mini waffle maker.
3. In a blender, combine well all the waffle ingredients.
4. When the waffle maker is ready, pour 1/2 of the batter.
5. Close the lid and cook 3 minutes.
6. Open the lid and flip the waffle. Place 1/2 of the cream cheese filling and raspberries in the center. Fold in half. Close the lid. (Do not push down.)  
7. Cook another 30 - 60 seconds with the lid ajar. 
8. Remove.
9. Wipe the waffle plate with a dry paper towel lightly if there's an overspill of the filling. Then, repeat with the remaining batter and filling.
10. Serve hot!

❋ **Approximate Nutritional Values Per Serving:**
Calories 155 kcal, Protein 5.4 g, Fat 13.6 g, Carbohydrate 2.1 g, Fiber 0.7 g, Sugar 1.2 g

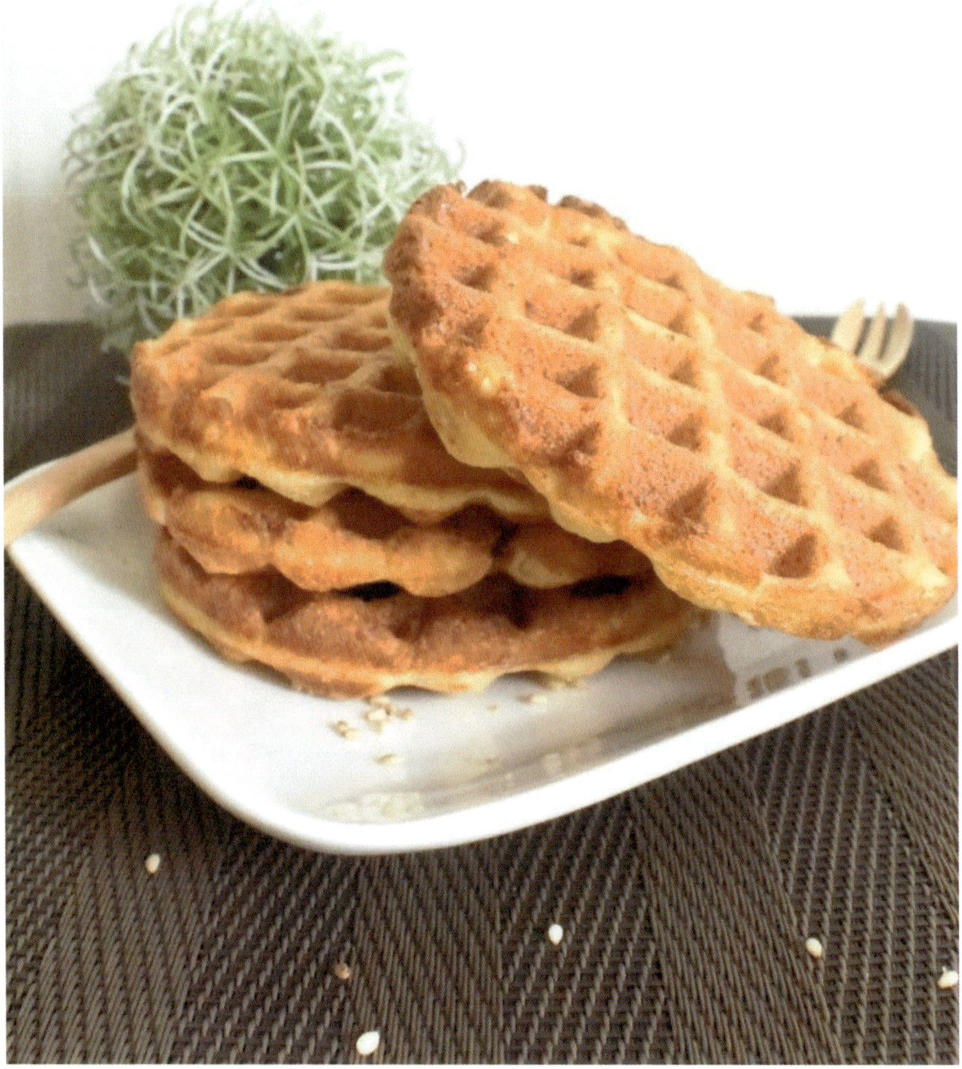

SESAME WAFFLE

Prep Time 3 minute
Cook Time 20 minutes
Total Time 23 minutes
Servings 4 waffles

✲ Ingredients
- 2 Eggs, Room Temp
- 1 oz (28 g) Cream Cheese, Softened
- 1 oz (28 g) Shredded Mozzarella Cheese
- 1 tbsp Tahini
- 2 tsp Ground Sesame Seeds
- 1 tbsp Heavy Cream
- 1 tbsp Mayonnaise
- 2 tsp Toasted Sesame Seeds

✲ Instructions
1. Preheat your mini waffle maker.
2. In a blender, combine well all the ingredients except for the toasted sesame seeds.
3. Add the toasted sesame seeds and stir lightly with a spoon.
4. When the waffle maker is ready, pour 1/4 of the batter. (Oil up with sesame oil if desired.)
5. Close the lid and cook 5 minutes. Then remove with tongs.
6. Repeat with the remaining batter.

✲ Recipe Notes
This Sesame Waffle is definitely one of my favorite keto waffles! The toasted sesame flavor is amazing.

Don't know what to do with Tahihi? Then, make **Sesame Dressing**! It goes well with salad, cooked vegetables such as broccoli and green beans, and chicken and pork.

Mix well the following ingredients in a bowl:
- 2 tbsp Tahini
- 1 tsp Sesame Oil
- 1/2 - 1 tsp Gluten Free Soy Sauce
- 1/2 tsp Apple Cider Vinegar
- 2 - 3 Drops Liquid Stevia
- Optional: 1 - 3 tsp Water (Adjust)

✲ Approximate Nutritional Values Per Serving:
Calories 152 kcal, Protein 7.0 g, Fat 13.0 g, Carbohydrate 1.8 g, Fiber 0.8 g, Sugar 0.9 g

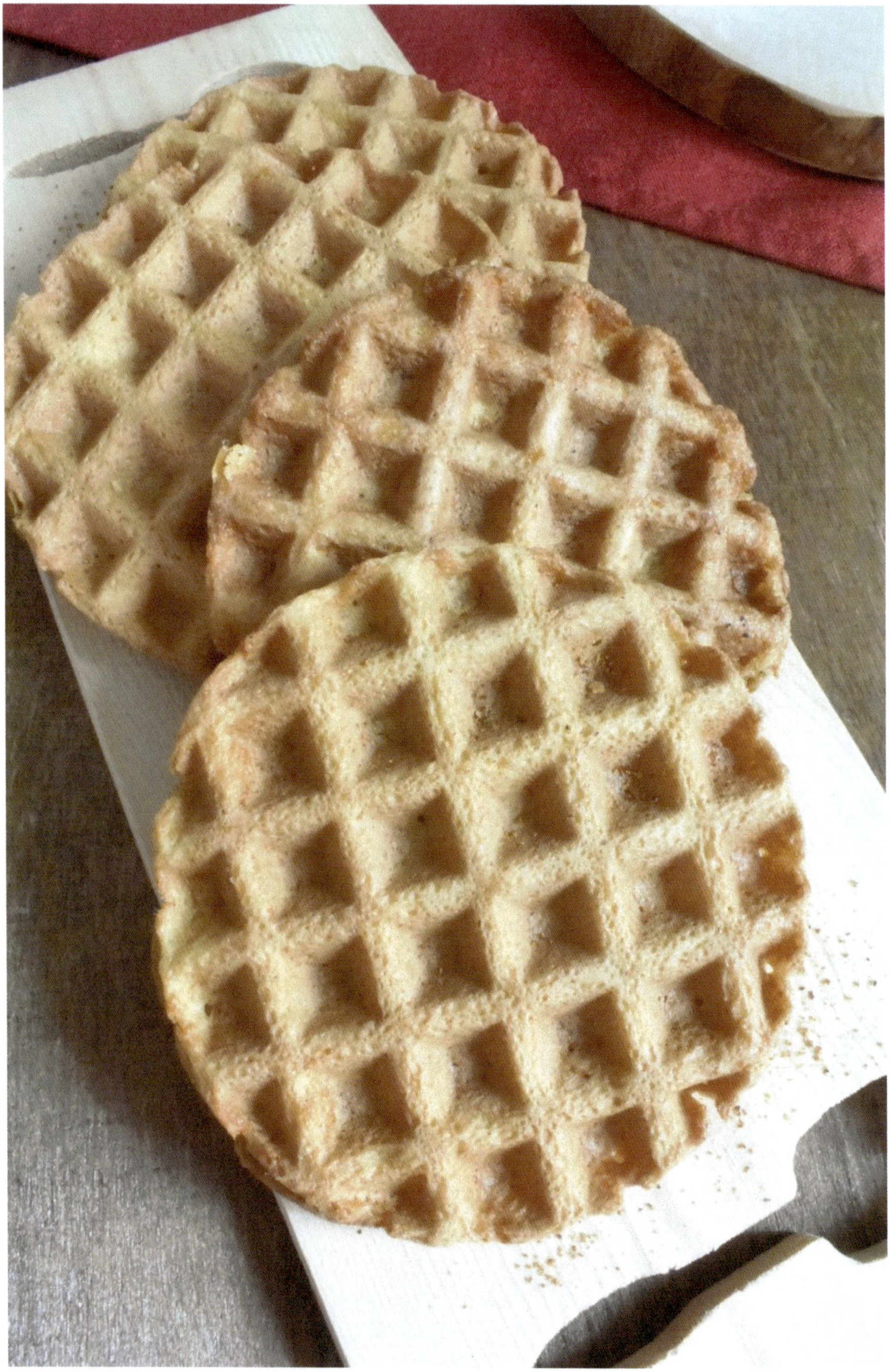

NACHO CHEESE WAFFLE

Prep Time 3 minute
Cook Time 20 minutes
Total Time 23 minutes
Servings 4 waffles

✱ Ingredients
- 1 Eggs, Room Temp
- 1 Egg White, Room Temp
- 1.5 oz (42 g) Shredded Red Cheddar Cheese
- 0.75 oz (21 g) Finely Grated Parmesan Cheese (About 3 tbsp)
- 1 tbsp Almond Flour
- 1 tsp Mayonnaise
- 1/2 tsp Garlic Powder
- 1/2 tsp Chili Powder
- 1/4 tsp Onion Powder
- 1/4 tsp Cumin Powder
- 1/4 tsp Smoked Paprika Powder
- A Pinch Sea Salt

✱ Instructions
1. Preheat your mini waffle maker.
2. In a blender, combine well all the ingredients.
3. When the waffle maker is ready, pour 1/4 of the batter.
4. Close the lid and cook 4 – 5 minutes. Then remove with tongs.
5. Repeat with the remaining batter.

✱ **Recipe Notes**
You can use egg whites only for a crispier texture. I used one whole egg because my mini waffle maker can't handle batter with egg whites only. It always sticks.

✱ **Approximate Nutritional Values Per Serving:**
Calories 137 kcal, Protein 10.3 g, Fat 9.8 g, Carbohydrate 0.8 g, Fiber 0.2 g, Sugar 0.5 g

KEEMA CURRY WAFFLE

Prep Time 5 minutes
Cook Time 30 minutes
Total Time 35 minutes
Servings 4

✱ **Ingredients**

Waffles
- 3 oz (85 g) Shredded Mozzarella Cheese
- 2 Eggs, Room Temp
- 3 tbsp Almond Flour
- 1/2 tsp Aluminum Free Baking Powder
- 1/4 tsp Garlic Powder

Keema Curry
- 10.5 oz (300 g) Ground Meat
- 1 tbsp Avocado Oil
- 1/4 tsp Salt
- 1/2 tsp Garlic Powder (Can use grated fresh garlic)
- 1/4 tsp Ginger Powder (Can use grated fresh ginger)
- 1/2 cup (120 cc) Tomato Puree
- 2 tbsp Worcestershire Sauce
- 2 tbsp Curry Powder

Topping
- 4 tsp Finely Grated Parmesan Cheese

✱ Instructions

Keema Curry
1. In a frying pan, cook the avocado oil over medium high heat.
2. Add the meat and cook until browned.
3. Add the salt, garlic powder, and ginger powder. Stir.
4. Add the tomato puree and Worcestershire sauce. Stir.
5. Add the curry powder and stir well. Then simmer 6 - 10 minutes over low heat.

Waffles (Makes 4 waffles)
1. Preheat your mini waffle maker.
2. In a small mixing bowl, whisk together all the ingredients except for the cheese.
3. When the waffle maker is ready, sprinkle 1/8 of the cheese and let melt.
4. (You may need to work a bit fast.) Pour 1/4 of the batter on top of the melted cheese. Spread 2 teaspoons of the keema curry and then sprinkle the same amount of cheese. Close the lid and cook 4 minutes. 
5. Remove with tongs.
6. Repeat with the remaining until you have 4 waffles.

Assembly
1. Place the remaining keema curry evenly on top of each waffle. (Reheat your keema curry if desired.)
2. Sprinkle one teaspoon of the Parmesan cheese on each (or any topping of your choice).

✱ Recipe Notes
You can of course serve this keema curry with fried cauliflower rice, not necessarily with waffles.

If desired, place shredded cheese on top instead of parmesan and put your keema curry waffle in a toaster oven and cook until melted.

Because of curry powder, cooked waffles may have burnt black spots. If you don't like that, you can simply cook your waffles without adding keema curry and use it all for placing on top of your waffles.

✱ Approximate Nutritional Values Per Serving (Half Beef Half Pork):
Calories 374 kcal, Protein 27.3 g, Fat 25.3 g, Carbohydrate 8.6 g, Fiber 2.4 g, Sugar 4.9 g

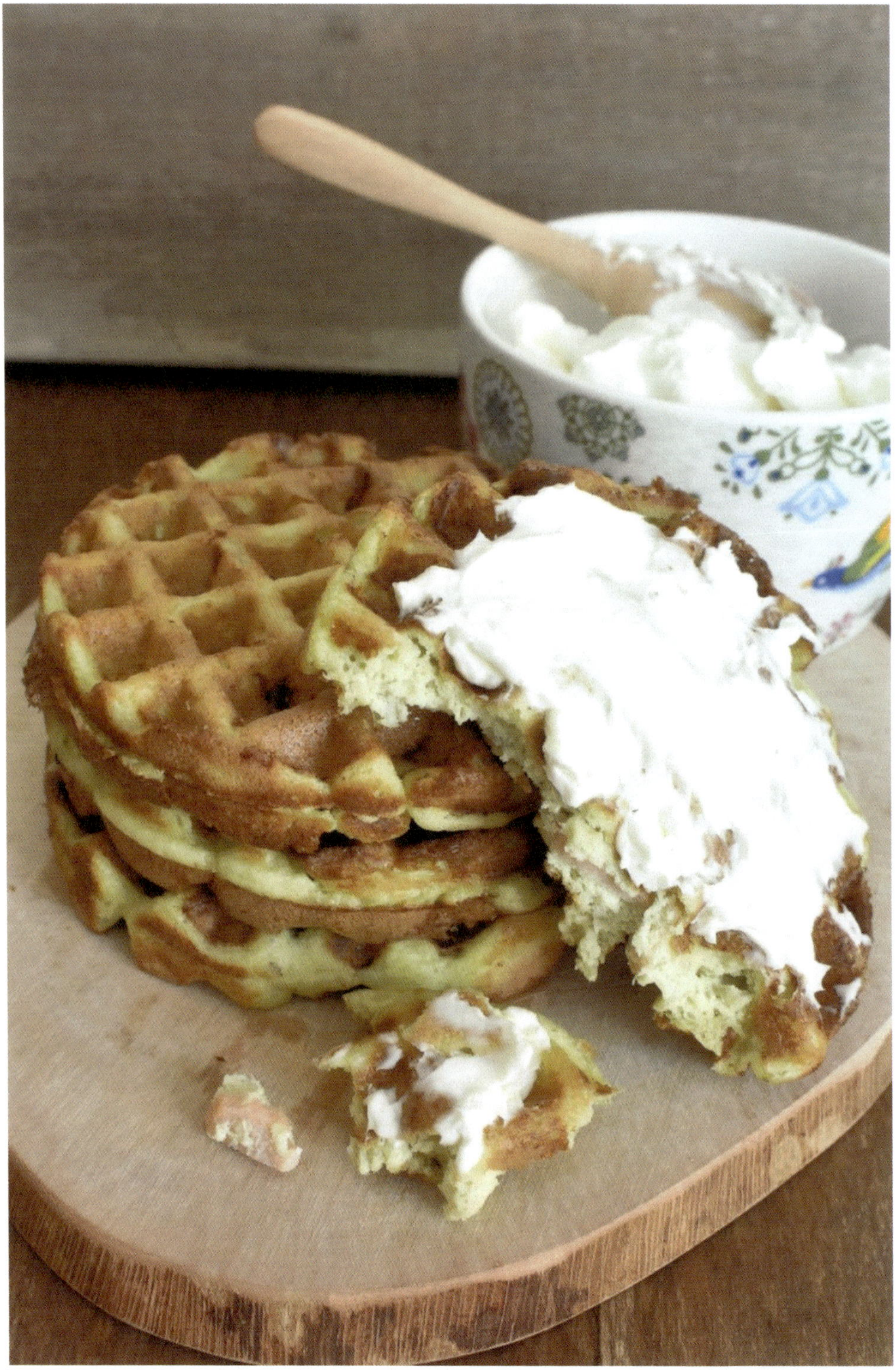

SALMON AVOCADO WAFFLE

Prep Time 5 minutes
Cook Time 16 minutes
Total Time 21 minutes
Servings 4

❋ **Ingredients**

Waffles
- 2 Eggs, Room Temp
- 1 oz (28 g) Shredded Mozzarella Cheese
- 1 oz (28 g) Cream Cheese, Softened
- 4 tbsp Almond Flour
- 1 tbsp Mayonnaise
- 1 tbsp Heavy Cream
- 1/2 Ripe Avocado
- 1 oz (28 g) Smoked Salmon, Chopped

Topping
- 4 tbsp Cream Cheese

❋ **Instructions**

1. Preheat your mini waffle maker.
2. In a blender, combine well all the ingredients except for the smoked salmon. Add the smoked salmon and stir lightly with a spoon.
3. When the waffle maker is ready, spoon 1/4 of the batter. Close the lid and cook 4 minutes.
4. Remove with tongs.
5. Repeat with the remaining until you have 4 waffles.
6. To serve, spread one tablespoon of the cream cheese on each waffle.

❋ **Approximate Nutritional Values Per Serving:**
Calories 252 kcal, Protein 10.8 g, Fat 21.8 g, Carbohydrate 3.7 g, Fiber 1.6 g, Sugar 1.3 g

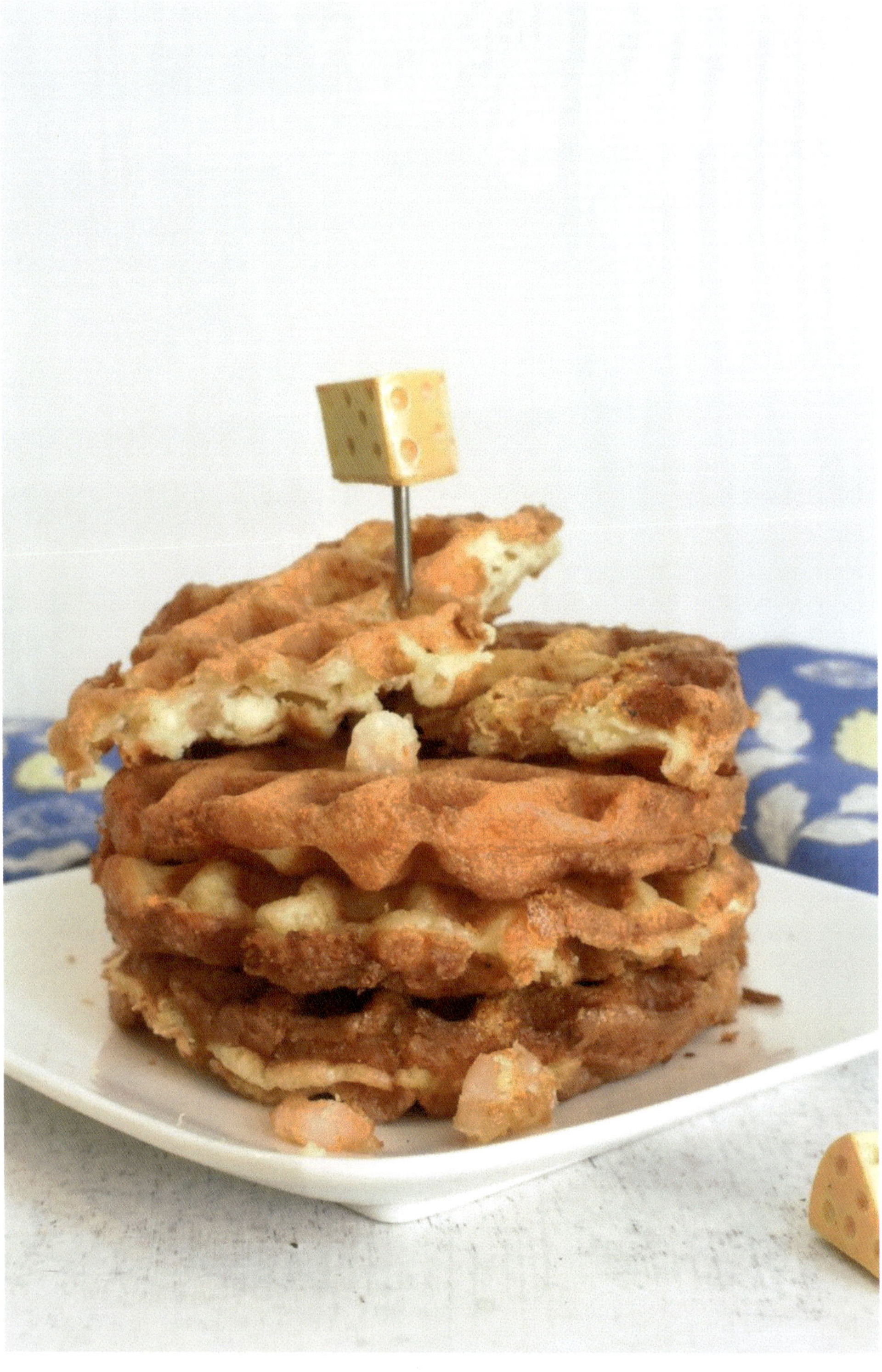

GARLIC SHRIMP WAFFLE

Prep Time 3 minutes
Cook Time 30 minutes
Total Time 33 minutes
Servings 5 waffles

✽ **Ingredients**

Waffles
- 1 Egg
- 2 Egg Whites
- 1.5 oz (42 g) Shredded Mozzarella Cheese
- 1.5 oz (42 g) Finely Grated Parmesan Cheese
- 2 tbsp Almond Flour
- 1 tbsp Mayonnaise
- 1 tbsp Heavy Cream

Garlic Shrimp
- 3 oz (85 g) Peeled & Deveined Shrimp
- 1 tsp Butter
- 1 clove Garlic, Minced
- A Pinch Salt
- A Pinch Black Pepper

✽ **Instructions**

Garlic Shrimp
1. Place the shrimp in a small bowl. Sprinkle the salt and black pepper and mix well with hands.
2. In a frying pan over low heat, melt the butter.
3. Add the minced garlic. Cook for one minute and turn the heat to medium. Add the shrimp and cook until pink.
4. Chop the shrimp into small pieces.

Waffles (Makes 5 waffles)
1. Preheat your mini waffle maker.
2. Whisk together all the waffle ingredients except for the mozzarella. Then, add the mozzarella and stir lightly.
3. When the waffle maker is ready, spoon 1/5 of the batter. Place 1/5 of the shrimp. Close the lid and cook 4 – 5 minutes. (Push down the lid of your waffle iron for several seconds while cooking. Egg whites make them puff up.)
4. Remove with tongs.
5. Repeat with the remaining until you have 5 waffles.

✽ **Recipe Notes**

It may be just my waffle maker, but you may need to oil up your waffle maker for this recipe. They taste great as is, but spreading a little bit of mayo and cooking in a toaster oven is also recommended!

✽ **Approximate Nutritional Values Per Serving:**
Calories 166 kcal, Protein 12.5 g, Fat 11.8 g, Carbohydrate 1.7 g, Fiber 0.4 g, Sugar 1.0 g

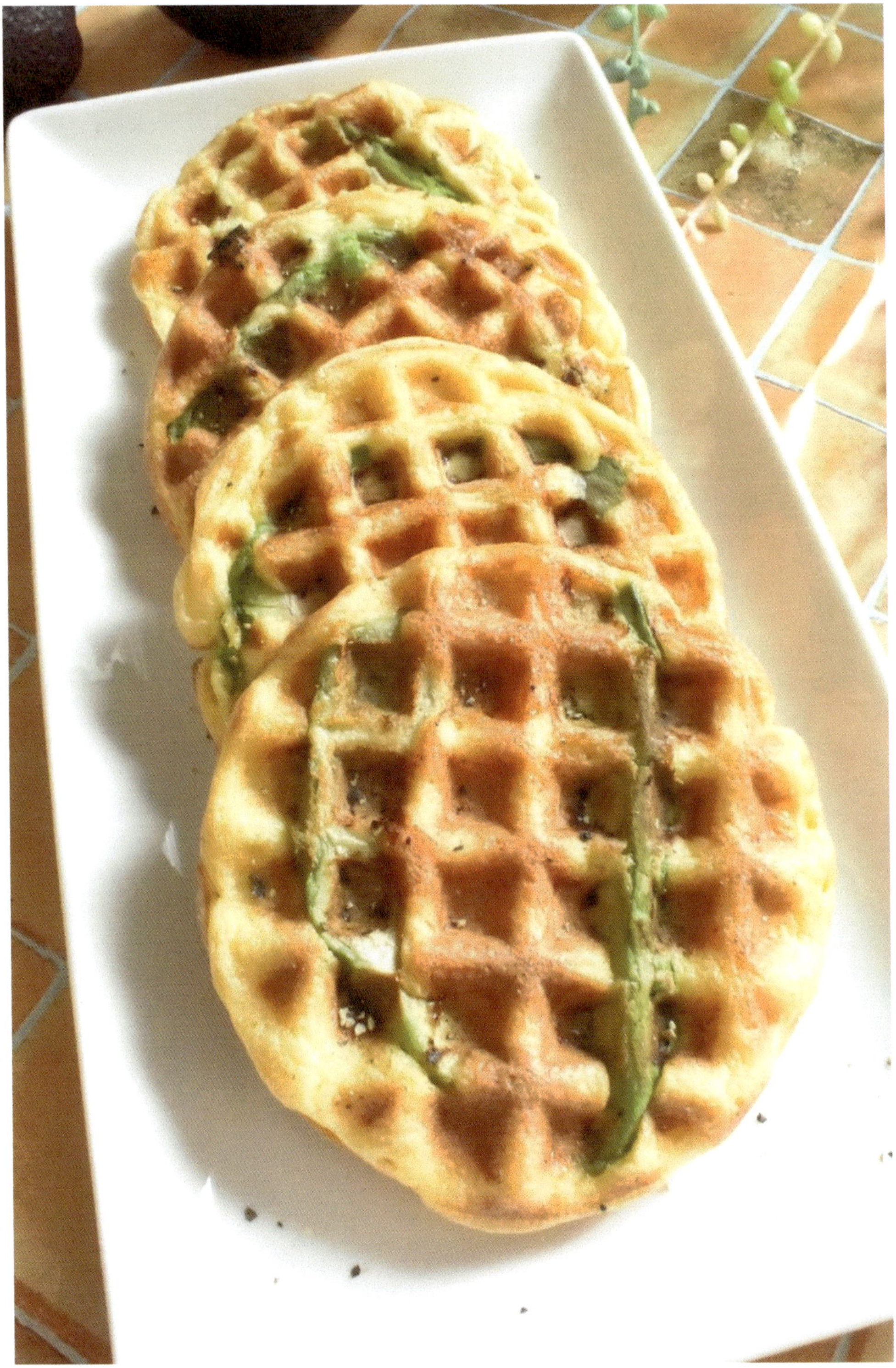

AVOCADO WAFFLE

Prep Time 5 minute
Cook Time 20 minutes
Total Time 25 minutes
Servings 4 waffles

❋ Ingredients

- 1/2 Ripe Avocado
- 2 Eggs, Room Temp
- 1 oz (28 g) Shredded Mozzarella Cheese
- 1 oz (28 g) Shredded Red Cheddar Cheese
- 1 tbsp Almond Flour
- 2 tbsp Mayonnaise
- 1 tbsp Heavy Cream
- 1/2 tsp Garlic Powder
- 1/4 tsp Black Pepper

❋ Instructions

1. Slice the avocado into 8 pieces.
2. Preheat your mini waffle maker.
3. In a bowl, whisk well all the ingredients except for the avocado slices.
4. When the waffle maker is ready, pour 1/4 of the batter. Place 2 avocado slices.
5. Close the lid and cook 4 – 5 minutes. Then remove with tongs.
6. Repeat with the remaining batter and avocado slices.

❋ **Approximate Nutritional Values Per Serving:**
Calories 180 kcal, Protein 7.7 g, Fat 15.7 g, Carbohydrate 2.1 g, Fiber 1.0 g, Sugar 0.8 g

Printed in Great Britain
by Amazon